SPENDING GOD'S MONEY

By

Mary Kinney Branson

Dedication

to the many
honest and hardworking
North American Mission Board staff
who kept their focus

to

Taylor and Elliott LeBaron:

Give what you can't keep
Gain what you can't lose[1]

---

[1] Christian martyr Jim Elliot

Cover design: Jennifer Rosania

Mary Kinney Branson can be contacted at:

> www.aptword.net

First printing, January 2007
© 2006 Mary Kinney Branson
Printed in the United States. All rights reserved.

ISBN 10: 0-9779407-6-4
ISBN 13: 978-0-9779407-6-9

Scriptures marked NIV are taken from the *Holy Bible: New International Version*, copyright © 1973, 1978, 1984 by the International Bible Society. Used by permission of International Bible Society.

All rights reserved. No part of this publication may be reproduced, stored in retrieval system, or transmitted in any form or by any means—electronic, mechanical, photocopy, recording, or any other—except for brief quotations in printed reviews, without the prior permission of the publisher.

Father's Press, LLC
Lee's Summit, MO (816) 554-2156
E-Mail: fatherspress@yahoo.com
www.fatherspress.com
www.mikesmitley.com

Table of Contents

Introduction..4

Section 1   God's Model for Giving

    Chapter 1:   God's Plan for His Money.................9

    Chapter 2:   Who's Spending God's Money?..........15

Section 2   From Giving to Delegation

    Chapter 3:   A Heritage of Wise Leaders.............21

    Chapter 4:   What Happened?..........................27

Section 3   Where We Are Today

    Chapter 5:   Lobster in the Pot.........................37

    Chapter 6:   Hollywood Bob...........................45

    Chapter 7:   Six Cents Worth of Butter...............53

    Chapter 8:   Friends in High Places...................65

    Chapter 9:   Surpassing the Joneses, Competing with Kings...83

    Chapter 10:   Mistakes with Your Money............101

    Chapter 11:   Condoms and Cruises..................111

Section 4   The Ghost of Giving Future

Chapter 12:   Staying the Course……………………..117

Chapter 13:   Turning the Ship Around……………125

Chapter 14:   Call to Change………………………..131

Chapter 15:   Newsworthy…………………………135

Chapter 16:   A Plan……………………………..…147

Appendices……………………………………………...…153

Acknowledgements

This is a rare book. Few contributors want to be publicly recognized for their contributions.

And that's understandable since most people who left the North American Mission Board signed an agreement not to talk or write negatively about the agency or its leaders. What's not understandable is why a Christian agency felt a need to require such a gag document of its employees.

So current and former NAMB staff: You know who you are, and thank you for your contributions.

Most of all, thanks to my husband, Jack, the love of my life and my greatest encourager. He researched, proofed, and prayed for *Spending God's Money*.

I also want to thank my prayer partners Jen Rosania and Linda Haas. Each day I wrote, I knew they were praying.

And my Sunday School class at Concord Baptist Church—they've taught me so much about generous giving and ministry.

Thanks to Bobby Sunderland for his immense enthusiasm for getting this message out. He put so much time into the book because he believes the message, he's a friend, and because his mom worked for 30 cents an hour at Ben Franklin's and gave sacrificially to Southern Baptist mission offerings. Thanks to Bobby's mom and millions of others who gave us a legacy of generous giving.

A special thanks to Joe Westbury for the excellent reporting that first brought this story to light. And to the reporters and bloggers who never let the light go out.

Mega thanks to Mike Smitley and Father's Press for the enthusiasm and energy that got this book out quickly

And thanks to my family, who supports and loves me unconditionally—Jack, Mom, Penny, Dave, Taylor, and Elliott. They'll always be my biggest fans. I'd write if they were my only readers.

Introduction

> "They are shepherds who lack understanding;
> they all turn to their own ways,
> each seeks his own gain."
> – Isaiah 56:11, NIV

It all boils down to a simple formula: The extent of misuse is directly proportionate to the distance between the giver and the spender. If Christians are to fulfill the Great Commission, individuals must shorten the distance between their gifts and the recipients.

As a denominational employee, I have paid car payments and bought groceries with sacrificial gifts from Christians who gave their money "to the Lord." I laid down agency credit cards backed by nickels and dimes from preschoolers and tithes of elderly saints. I used this money, and I tried to use it wisely.

But I saw how easy it was to compete for my share of the funds and how hard it was to remember who provided the money and why. A wise leader once told me: "When you do the Lord's work every day, the Lord's work can become everyday work." I tried to guard against that, but I certainly wasn't perfect and I'm not drawing lines. I don't look at myself as a good guy and the people I describe in this book as the bad ones. I adhere to the adage that "there is so much bad in the best of us and so much good in the worst of us"—well, you know. No one has the right to point fingers.

I feel a little like Jonah, who would just as soon have stayed in Gath-hepher. Or Gideon, who preferred to hide in the threshing field. I tried for more than a year to ignore God's leading to write this book because I wasn't excited about casting stones. And on the human side, I'd seen the way powerful people can and will destroy those who stand in their paths.

But the leading just got stronger, and I knew I'd been placed in a unique position and given a somewhat unpleasant assignment.

Though I watched careful spending on the part of many dedicated Christian leaders, I also saw gross misuse of money given sacrificially by trusting churches and laypeople.

I saw firsthand—or heard from reliable sources—of ice sculptures for parties, a business retreat planned around a cruise to the Bahamas, private jets for travel, and millions paid to friends for business not sent out for bids.

I do not believe that the average giver envisions his or her money used for ice sculptures and private jets. When we write a check to a Christian charity or give through our church to a denominational agency, we often sacrifice to make the gift. We picture our money providing Bibles for people eager to hear God's Word. We envision food given to hungry people in the name of the Lord.

We imagine the type of hands-on giving we see in the local church: The food pantry has empty shelves, so everyone gives a couple of dollars to restock it. The youth plan a mission trip to Tanzania, and the senior adult class takes up money for their airplane tickets. We see a need, we meet it directly, and we see the results. Everyone involved receives a blessing.

But what would we do if we heard that the lady who stocks the food bank used most of the money to fly to New York and eat at Sardis, picking up a few canned goods on the way home? How would we feel if the youth director stopped off in Paris and used our money for a shopping spree on her way to Tanzania?

Somewhere between giving to giant faceless agencies and filling the need, a lot of money is misspent. Most parachurch groups and denominational agencies could be likened to extravagant middlemen in the retail business. Buying directly from the factory gives us more for our dollar.

Two thousand years ago, Jesus gave us the Great Commission, to go into all the world and preach the gospel to every person. Many have lost their lives obeying Jesus' command. We've spent billions of dollars trying to reach our world for Christ. But 2,000 years later, we're still far, far from the goal.

The population is growing faster than our evangelism efforts. We may wrestle with numbers to make it appear that we're successful, but we're losing ground when we face the percentages. It's not because the people in the pew aren't giving. Could it be because their sacrificial gifts are often blatantly misused?

The *Didaché*, an early church document that details the teachings of the Twelve Apostles, affirms the support of church leaders and so do I: "Every true prophet that wishes to abide among you is worthy of his support."[1] It's the definition of *support* that's gotten cloudy as bigger and more elaborate denominational agencies and para-church groups surface. Practical Christians realize that every dollar can't go for Bibles. Utility bills must be paid. Denominational workers' children need braces. Plane tickets to important meetings are costly.

But shouldn't more money be reaching a spiritually dying world?

Somewhere between the giver and the spender there often develops a spirit of entitlement—a feeling that God's servants are corporate CEOs who deserve nothing but the best.

A.W. Tozer said, "No matter the size of the assembly or its other attributes, our Lord wants it to be known by His presence in the midst. I would rather have His presence in the church than anything else in the wide world. Hearing the proud manner in which some speak of the high dollar cost of their sanctuaries must lead people to suppose that spirituality can be purchased."[2]

If we are to reach our world for Christ, *all* our leaders must begin measuring their worth by their relationship to God instead of their freedom to spend His money, with the most valued leaders being those with the greatest ability to raise

---

[1] Chapter 13, "Support of Prophets," published by P. Bryennios, 1883.
[2] "Failure and Success: Status Symbols," *Tozer on Christian Leadership: A 366-Day Devotional*, A.W. Tozer, Ronald E. Eggert (compiler), Christian Publications, Inc., 2001.

money and spend it. And we as individual believers must see that our tithes and offerings are spent as carefully as we spend our grocery budget. To do this, we must investigate the spending of those who spend on our behalf.

The more closely the giver is connected with the spender, the more carefully the spender is likely to spend. In the following pages, I offer a look at God's plan for giving and effective giving in the past, a scrutiny of current spending, and suggestions for making our giving count.

The message here is not that we should reduce our giving because of flagrant misuse. On the contrary, my plea is that we will all increase our giving. Time is short. The world needs the hope that only Jesus Christ can give. My message to you, the reader, is simply this: Take back the responsibility of giving.

God expects us to be good stewards, and I believe that includes knowing how our money is spent.

Just as the servant (Luke 12) is accountable to his master, we are accountable to God. If the servant had said, "Well, I took all the resources you gave me—the money, the employees, the land—and I handed them over to someone else. I never checked to see that the resources were managed properly, *but my intentions were good*" how do you think the master would have reacted?

Spending God's money has become big business, and I propose that it once again become a hands-on, personal, and dynamic expression of our love for Christ. It's not enough just to write a check. I believe that we'll someday give account for how the money was used. We're the stewards, and the buck stops with us.

—Mary Kinney Branson

Section 1   God's Model for Giving

Chapter 1
God's Plan for His Money

Most of us appreciate the story of the rich young ruler (Mark 10:17-31), but we may prefer to keep it in its biblical setting. It's difficult to apply to today's culture, where a person is measured not by his relationship with God but by the make and model of his car, the location of her house, and the size of his office.

Christian leaders aren't immune to these modern standards of worth. Pastors quiz each other about their Sunday School enrollments and compare annual budgets. Denominational leaders demand high salaries, company cars, and the trappings of other "CEOs." It's reminiscent of Lucy in *A Charlie Brown Christmas*: "All I want is my fair share. All I want is what's coming to me."

It's you and me who finance this unholy competition, and the further our leaders get from Jesus' teachings, the more we pay.

But that's not how God intended it to be, and the message to the rich young ruler is as powerful today as it was when Jesus gave His radical instructions to "sell everything you have and follow Me."

What Jesus told the young man was unthinkable, even 2,000 years ago, and the disciples were confused. Here was a man who could have financed their ministry. He'd just require some special attention. You know, give him a front-row seat when Jesus taught. Compliment his robe. Make sure his feet were washed and his head had a little oil.

But here was Jesus, treating him like everyone else. He wasn't showing him the admiration a rich man expected. Instead, He shocked them all with His blunt directive, "Go, sell everything you have and give it to the poor, and you'll have treasure in heaven."

Not surprisingly, the rich man left. Peter and the other disciples watched as he walked away, no doubt as disheartened as the ruler himself.

As the rich man walked away, Jesus made the ultimate absurd comment: "How hard it is for the rich to enter the kingdom of God!"

What?

Jesus continued, "It's easier for a camel to go through the eye of a needle than for a rich man to enter the kingdom of God."

Jesus was always surprising His disciples, but this was more than they could handle. Wasn't wealth an indication of God's favor? Those in high religious positions were always prosperous and powerful. What was Jesus saying? Had the rules changed?

If the rules had changed, it was man who changed them. Jesus' instructions to the rich young ruler were based on the ancient truth that Moses carried down the mountain on stone tablets: "Thou shalt have no other gods before me." You can't love money more than God. Your desire for money can't overshadow your desire for God, or you're not worthy of Him.

"Who then can be saved?" asked Peter. If the rich and influential couldn't make it to heaven, why were the rest of them trying? All their lives, they'd been taught that those who obeyed God were blessed with prosperity. And what was wrong with a little wealth? They didn't doubt that Jesus was from God, but sometimes His demands seemed so all-or-nothing, so unreasonable.

All or nothing

But that's the way God is. Each of us can put only one thing first in our lives. God gives us richly all things to enjoy (1 Tim. 6:17), and the only time these blessings are a problem is when they take first place.

The story of the rich young ruler is chock full of insights into the problems of 21st century ministry. First, there's the rich young ruler. He's done about everything you can think of to please God. Except give Him first place. In spite of that one major flaw, he's still held in the highest worldly esteem.

Then there are the disciples. They love Christ. They've even left everything to follow Him. But they just don't get it. They're still giving money the same honored place the rest of the world gives it. They want more money for themselves, and they're impressed by those who have lots of it.

And there's Jesus, who loves them all—loves *us* all—to the point of death on a cross. He doesn't mind confronting the rich young ruler because He knows the ruler's life depends on it. His goal is to teach the ruler, the disciples, and us that there's more to the kingdom of God than what this world offers.

As the story began, Jesus and the disciples were traveling south for the Passover. It was the beginning of what we now know was the final week of Christ's earthly life. Jesus knew His time on earth was short, and He took these last precious moments to teach us what really matters.

When the rich young ruler fell at Jesus' feet, he called Him "good teacher." Other rabbis reveled in such titles, but Jesus replied, "Why do you call Me good? No one is good—except God alone." If Jesus refused the title of "good," how can any of us hold up our filthy self-righteous rags and choose the stance of entitlement?

When Jesus reviewed the commandments, the young man replied with naïve honesty: "Teacher, I've kept all these commandments since I was a boy." Then why was he there? Something must have been missing or he wouldn't have sought out Jesus.

Jesus confronted the man's false confidence: "One thing you lack." Jesus challenged the man to get rid of the only thing that stood between him and his relationship with God. "Go, sell everything you have and give to the poor, and you will have treasure in heaven. Then come, follow Me."

This was not an exercise in "how high can you jump for God," and it wasn't a one-time test for a solitary man in Judea. It's a question each of us must ask ourselves constantly: Is there anything that's more important to us than God? It was not the rich man's wealth that kept him from God. It was the value he placed on it.

A week later, Jesus showed the world the true nature of God's kingdom. The heir to the heavenly throne, the owner of a thousand vineyards, the commander of 10 legions of angels gave up everything. He stood behind His words that the kingdom of God had nothing to do with earthly wealth. By His death and resurrection, Jesus showed us that there is more to the kingdom of God than what this world could ever offer.

Christ as commodity

But 2,000 years later, we still don't get it. We've come no farther than the rich young ruler. Materialism affects us all, and for most of us, it's the focus of nearly everything we do. But when it affects denominational leaders, everyone pays doubly. Our sacrificial gifts pay for luxuries you and I would never expect for ourselves. And the work for which our gifts were intended may be left undone.

Our churches, para-churches, and denominational headquarters include many dedicated men and women. They also include some "rich young rulers" who assume that their service entitles them to the very best of this life. They live in a spirit of entitlement, assuming that their positions warrant Armani suits and luxury vehicles.

It's sad that these leaders may end up missing the reason for their existence, but it's equally tragic that the dollars they squander are the dollars you and I intended for the Lord's work.

When leaders believe that affluence is a perk of ministry, affluence becomes a snare that blinds them to the will of God. Believers should find it disconcerting that some major modern-day ministries are no longer evaluated according to the power of God through them or the Christ-likeness of the disciples they train. Instead, they are often measured (at least internally and by fellow ministries) by the size of their budgets and the living standards of their highest-ranking leaders.

Some "ministries" make Christ a commodity. They mix secular business with sacred guidelines. They use the world as their measurement of success.

Like the rich young ruler, too many of our leaders have gotten it backwards. Wealth is not proof that God is blessing our efforts in ministry. God's presence is evidence of His blessings. And only when we empty ourselves of the world can God fill us with His presence.

Most of us agree that we cannot address a problem until we acknowledge that the problem exists. In this case, the problem can be carefully hidden in a cloak of piety and religious clichés. On the surface, leaders do what we expect them to do. They tell us what we want to hear.

And often we don't want to examine the situation too closely. If we're faced with the misuse of our money, we're confronted with a call to action. And that gets complicated because we're busy people who would prefer to write a check and go on with our lives.

It is not enough to console ourselves that our intent was good. God holds us accountable not only for writing the check, but also for who cashes it and how the money is used. After giving, sometimes sacrificially, who knows if 1 Corinthians 3:12-15 (NIV) may someday pertain to our giving through secondary sources that misused our funds: "If any man builds on this foundation using gold, silver, costly stones, wood, hay or straw, his work will be shown for what it is, because the Day will bring it to light. It will be revealed with fire, and the fire will test the quality of each man's work. If what he has built survives, he will receive his reward. If it is burned up, he will suffer loss; he himself will be saved, but only as one escaping through the flames."

Chapter 2
Who's Spending God's Money?

Good intentions

In 1845, when travel and communication were difficult, Southern Baptists began cooperating to send missionaries to the field. But most of the fundraising was done by the missionaries themselves. They took time away from their work, traveled halfway back around the world, and told their story in hundreds of rural churches. Then they sent churches' offerings back to a main office, where they were distributed according to need. What one individual or church couldn't do alone, an army of givers could do with ease. From that concept, the Cooperative Program was born.[3]

By 1925, Southern Baptists had revolutionized their giving and multiplied their efforts by asking churches to simply send a portion of their undesignated funds directly to the main SBC office and take missionaries out of the primary fundraising strategy. Now, more than 43,000 Southern Baptist churches give regularly to CP, to the tune of nearly half a billion dollars annually.[4]

For years, CP made it possible for small churches to be part of sending missionaries to distant countries and obscure parts of the United States. It was a great idea whose time had come.

---

[3] The SBC national giving strategy that allows churches to pool their resources for major evangelism and ministry efforts, including support of the International Mission Board and the North American Mission Board.
[4] $499 million in 2004, with nearly $190 million going for national and international costs, per www.cpmissions.net.

Intentions gone awry

Perhaps now, its time has passed. With improved communication, transportation, and technology, today's small churches can easily be involved in mission causes around the world. And the Cooperative Program now supports astronomical salaries for agency CEOs, maintenance of huge agency office buildings, and programs that are duplicated in state conventions, associations, and local churches (evangelism, children's homes, volunteer missions, mission education, new churches). CP also supports Southern Baptist seminaries (which, in turn, have their own colleges and universities), but these institutions still have high tuition costs.[5]

With recipients of CP funds spread across the world, scrutinizing spending is difficult, and funds can easily be misused. In February 2006, the *Christian Index*[6] published an article that revealed some of the appalling misuses of CP dollars, focusing on the CP-supported North American Mission Board and its president Bob Reccord.[7] I'd worked at NAMB since it began in 1997 (and before that, at its predecessor, the Home Mission Board). I was NAMB's first woman director, and I left in 2004 under positive circumstances.[8] But I left with memories of extravagance and misuse of CP dollars—dollars that came from sacrificial gifts from churches and individuals.

Two months after the *Index* article, Bob stepped down as president, taking a lawyer into his "transition negotiations." Word soon spread that he left the meeting with a half million dollars in severance, a two-year total benefits package, and at

---

[5] www.cpmissions.net. Also check out tuition costs on individual seminary websites.

[6] Georgia's state Baptist paper.

[7] "North America: Hanging in the Balance," by Joe Westbury, with additional reporting by J. Gerald Harris, *The Christian Index*, February 16, 2006.

[8] See Appendix 1 for affirming emails from NAMB's president, chief operating officer, and my vice president when I announced I was leaving.

least $12,000 to pay a head hunter to find him a new job. All paid, I assume, with CP dollars.

When it became known that I was writing this book, I was contacted by scores of former and current NAMB staff. I heard stories of misuse at other CP-supported entities, including a story of one SBC leader who had his ailing dog airlifted to a veterinarian and charged his CP-supported entity for the roundtrip helicopter ride. I heard from a former International Mission Board (CP-supported) missionary how IMB trustees traveled to Africa to observe her work. While most found time to go on a safari, only two observed her classroom, and one of them slept through the entire class.

One knowledgeable current NAMB staff member commented, "Bob Reccord didn't do anything that other SBC leaders don't do. He just wasn't savvy enough to hide his spending. Others would have coded a trip to London to watch a movie as 'visiting chaplaincy sites.' He was so enamored with being invited to the premiere of *The Chronicles of Narnia* that he bragged about it." This same person described another well-known CP-supported leader as "Bob on steroids."

The problem with Bob was not an isolated one. While the Cooperative Program still does many good things, the purpose for which it was designed is, in some cases, now lost.

The power structure

And no one knows this better than the handful of powerful men who run the Southern Baptist Convention. My pastor, Dan Armistead, recently summed up the SBC power structure: "When conservatives won the battle for the Bible[9] they rewarded themselves with power. And now they protect that power."

---

[9] He referred to the conservative resurgence, starting in 1979, when conservatives took back power in the Southern Baptist Convention by making sure that the majority of denominational leaders and board members were conservative.

These leaders—some estimate their number to be about 35[10]—make many SBC decisions in restaurants and motel rooms long before motions are officially made on the floor of the annual Convention. This small group of powerful leaders are the ones spending the money for more than 16 million Southern Baptists. Each year we give them millions and millions of sacrificial dollars and trust them to spend God's money wisely.

Who's spending God's money?

But the startling fact is that the very leaders spending our money don't give much to the Cooperative Program themselves. Occasionally, an SBC president is a strong CP giver, but apparently CP giving has historically had no bearing on whether a pastor is chosen to spend CP dollars.

One of the first names that surfaced for 2006 SBC president was Johnny Hunt, whose church gave a paltry percentage to CP. He was also one of the 41 SBC leaders (mostly mega pastors) who signed a statement affirming Bob Reccord's actions after a trustee investigation revealed undisputed misuse of funds. As word spread that an ad hoc CP committee would be encouraging "the election of state and

---

[10] The applicable part of the article: "In the past 25 years, the convention has been run like an oligarchy. A former president of Southeastern Baptist Theological Seminary, Randall Lolley, once told me that he estimated the convention was in the hands of about 35 people. Even if this is an overstatement, it is clear that there is an inner circle making most of the decisions.

"This is truly strange for the Southern Baptists, who historically have prided themselves on their form of direct democracy, which at their conventions could be rather freewheeling. But for the past several years, the convention's agenda has been so tightly controlled that no surprises have been permitted, even from otherwise friendly conservatives who happen to be outside the power structure. So bland and predictable have the conventions become that most major secular newspapers and networks have quit covering them." The April 1, 2006, article is written by Cary McMullen, religion editor for Lakeland, Florida's *Ledger*.

national convention officers whose churches give at least 10 percent of their undesignated receipts through the Cooperative Program"[11] at the upcoming annual meeting, Hunt deflected the spotlight from his own church and instead nominated Ronnie Floyd as SBC president.

Floyd's church gave .27 percent to CP. Less than a third of a percent. Yet he was willing and ready to oversee the sacrificial gifts from churches and individuals giving 10 percent or more. Sixteen million of us. Trusting our money to a handful of people tattooed with "do as I say, not as I do."

In a guest commentary in the May 25, 2006, *Christian Index*, Mike Stone, senior pastor of Emmanuel Baptist Church, Blackshear, Ga., stated, "In thousands of churches this fall, faithful pastors will face skeptical finance committees at budget preparation time. He will go out to bat to keep CP giving strong even in light of building programs and tight budgets. The last thing that warrior needs is for his finance committee chairman to ... read that Southern Baptists elected a president whose church gave .27 percent." I think it's just as bad that such a person could be nominated by a powerful SBC leader.

Getting it right

If we're going to win our world for Christ, we have to get our priorities straight. We must get on board with God's plan for spending His money. We must realize the gravity of such spending, and we can't blindly turn that responsibility over to others.

We cannot be like the rich young ruler, whose pillar of strength was his money, with God as the decoration. He must come first, and His work must be so important that we take an active part in knowing how our money is spent. To make Jesus Christ and His work first in our lives is simply smart thinking.

---

[11] "You can't spell 'SBC president' without the 'C' and the 'P,'" *The Christian Index*, May 25, 2006.

Jim Elliot said it best. In the 29 years before he died a martyr's death in 1956 at the hands of Ecuadorian Indians he was seeking to lead to Christ, he came to understand: "He is no fool who gives what he cannot keep to gain what he cannot lose."[12]

---

[12] Billy Graham Center, http://www.wheaton.edu/bgc/archives/faq/20.htm.

Section 2   From Giving to Delegation

Chapter 3
A Heritage of Wise Leaders

Most of what I know about good and not-so-good leaders comes from my personal experience. I was children's minister for a large Southern Baptist church for nearly six years, and I served at the Southern Baptist Home Mission Board and North American Mission Board for 16 years, primarily as editing director and marketing director. You'll find references to my experiences with these organizations generously sprinkled throughout these pages.

The Law of the Lid

I believe God set high standards for leaders because He knew we would never rise above the level of those we follow. It's what John Maxwell calls "The Law of the Lid,"[13] and that law applies to responsible use of finances. The leader sets the standard.

When questions began to surface in 2006 about presidential misuse of funds at the North American Mission Board, a little digging revealed that the president wasn't the only one with questionable financial practices. Almost immediately, three upper-level employees (including the chief operating officer) were dismissed or quietly resigned. Word soon spread that two of the three had produced a product while at NAMB, had it copyrighted in their name, and were using

---

[13] *The 21 Irrefutable Laws of Leadership*, John Maxwell, with Foreword by Zig Ziglar, Nelson Business, 1998.

NAMB money to purchase it from themselves. The other had supposedly set up a business in his home and was literally outsourcing to himself.

While not everyone played the Lucy card ("All I want is my fair share"), the climate was inviting for opportunistic people who saw the president's outside book deals and near-weekly personal speaking engagements and thought, "It must be OK to have businesses on the side."

That's why guidelines should be tough for leaders. Their behavior dominoes.

First Corinthians 9:9-19 gives us a clue to why responsible Christian leadership is so difficult. It's sort of like dieting as opposed to quitting smoking. Though I'm sure it's difficult to do, you control smoking by telling yourself, "I will never smoke another cigarette." Then you either smoke or you don't.

Dieting is more of a tightrope. You can't promise never to eat again. Sooner or later, you'll have to pull a chair up to the table. And then you have choices to make: Which foods should you have and how much should you have of each one?

Money, for Christian leaders, is like food to a dieter. These Corinthian verses say that the law (referring to Deut. 25:4) tells us not to muzzle an ox when he's working in a corn field. He's entitled to food to sustain him for his work. In other words, Christian leaders are permitted to make a living preaching the gospel. So just like a dieter and food, decisions must be made.

Now the question becomes: What's reasonable financial remuneration, what's legal but lacking integrity, and what's out-and-out dishonest and greedy behavior?

Paul was clear (vv. 10-14) that "those who preach the gospel should live of the gospel." In other words, pastors, other church staff, and denominational leaders deserve a reasonable salary. Having served on a church staff and as a denominational worker, I know my salary never seemed enough. I've always believed that we should pay our leaders fairly.

Up through verse 14, I can hear the religious wheeler dealers saying, "See, God expects me to live well if I preach the gospel." But verse 15 stops what could sound like an open door to financial extravagance. "BUT," says Paul. He continues in so many words, "I haven't used this guaranteed income because I'd rather die than do anything that takes glory from God. I have to preach the gospel, no matter what, and my reward is bringing glory to God."

In verse 18, Paul summarizes in one phrase his feelings about his involvement with God's money: "that I abuse not my power in the gospel." Some things were available to Paul because he preached the gospel, but he would rather take nothing at all than put a cloud of dishonesty, extravagance, or waste over God's work.

God used Paul to set an incredible example of integrity. Believers can follow his legacy with confidence.

Through the next couple of millennia, a parade of Christian leaders lived and died. We treasure the ones who lived extraordinary, sacrificial lives. The others either stand out as horrid examples or are now as forgotten as the material possessions they based their existence on. Surely there were Jim and Tammy Fayes in earlier generations, with less sophisticated equivalents to air-conditioned dog houses, but they're now forgotten.

The individuals who still inspire us are those who led and served with humility. When we remember them, we want to be better people.

One we remember

Southern Baptists stand high on the shoulders of a woman who, herself, stood just 4 feet 3 inches tall. This lady, born in 1840, is still a standard by which we can measure sacrificial giving.

Lottie Moon came from a privileged Virginia family. She once described herself as "overindulged and under-disciplined." Her family valued education in an era when few women had opportunities for higher education. Lottie's sister,

Orianna, became a physician. Lottie earned both bachelor's and master's degrees and became a teacher and assistant principal.

Wealthy and educated, she—like Paul—had reason for earthly boasting (Phil. 3:4-7). She could have lived a life of extravagance, but she chose a bank account in heaven (Matt. 6:20). When God called her to go to China as a missionary, she left not only her comfortable lifestyle but also the family environment where independent, educated women were applauded. She entered a world of poverty where women's feet, as well as their spirits, were bound.

Most 19th century missionaries were married men, and mission policies limited the work women could do. But at the age of 33, Lottie moved to China, following another sister, Eddie, and worked tirelessly to open doors for women missionaries to have greater opportunities for service.

Lottie could have spent her life wearing elegant gowns and relaxing in her family home in Virginia. Instead she wore Chinese clothing and became more concerned about reaching people for Christ than impressing others with her lavish lifestyle. The more she lived like the Chinese, the more she identified with them and loved them.

Lottie took only two furloughs during her years as a missionary—one after 19 years of service and another 10 years later. When she returned to China after her second furlough, she faced a war-torn country where people were starving all around her.

Lottie wrote home, begging for money and resources, but the mission board was heavily in debt. They could send nothing and, in fact, missionaries were asked to take voluntary pay cuts.

Lottie shared her food and resources with the Chinese people. Often she went without eating so someone else could have a meal. Her physical and mental health declined. Her weight dropped to 50 pounds, but still she sacrificed for the people she loved.

In 1912, her fellow missionaries arranged for Lottie to return to the United States. After a few days onboard a ship, her friends doubted she'd make it to America. One day, after gaining a little strength by drinking some juice, she and a friend whispered the words of "Jesus Loves Me."

The next morning, Lottie could no longer speak. But she pointed toward heaven as a nurse cared for her. The ship docked at Kobe, Japan, to take on coal. It was Christmas Eve 1912. Lottie opened her eyes and looked around. She smiled and, with her last bit of strength, she placed her fists together and raised them in a joyous Chinese greeting. Those who saw her thought she was greeting the Lord because, at that moment, He took His servant home.

That Christmas Eve, at the age of 72, Lottie Moon literally died of starvation onboard a ship in a Japanese harbor. Southern Baptists named their international missions offering, given during the Christmas season, after this great lady: The Lottie Moon Christmas Offering for International Missions.

Lottie's one of the good guys, one whose sacrifice still impacts and inspires us. She understood true servant leadership, even before the phrase was popular. She spent her entire inheritance and her entire life giving not just wisely but with total abandon.

She once wrote: "I wonder how many of us really believe that it is more blessed to give than to receive. A woman who accepts that statement of our Lord Jesus Christ as a fact and not as 'impractical idealism,' will make giving a principle of her life. She will lay aside sacredly not less than one-tenth of her income or her earnings as the Lord's money, which she would no more dare touch for personal use than she would steal. How many there are among our women, alas, who imagine that because 'Jesus paid it all,' they need pay nothing, forgetting that the prime object of their salvation was that they should follow in the footsteps of Jesus Christ!"[14]

Lottie's words and actions give us the path to follow: the footsteps of Jesus Christ. It is the wise heritage available to us and to our leaders.

---

[14] From the International Mission Board website's biography of Lottie Moon: www.imb.org.

Chapter 4
What Happened?

Years passed. The same Southern Baptists who named an offering after Lottie Moon managed home missions (missions in the United States and its territories) through their headquarters in Atlanta. Home mission leaders were appointed, they retired, and new leaders were appointed.

Occasionally, dishonest leaders surfaced, and their actions became a reminder that evil slips in when we step off the path of following Jesus' footsteps. When I came to the Home Mission Board (the predecessor of the North American Mission Board) in 1988, a tour of the Heritage Room was part of my employee orientation. This room held mementos of the agency.

These mementos included a corporate seal with the name of a shell (fake) company. The seal was used by an HMB financial executive to funnel money from the HMB to his private account. By the time his dishonesty was discovered, the agency was financially distressed. Southern Baptists across the nation partnered to rebuild the board's finances, and the seal was displayed in the Heritage Room as a reminder to guard our hearts and footsteps.

When the North American Mission Board was formed in 1997, there was no Heritage Room. Instead, the agency built a $1+ million Vision Center. Bob Reccord, the president, had visited Focus on the Family, liked their Visitors Center, and decided he needed one, too. In late 1998, Chuck Allen, a NAMB executive who later became chief operating officer, was assigned by Bob to build a NAMB Vision Center and have it ready for visitors when the Southern Baptist Convention met in Atlanta in June 1999. As marketing director, I was assigned to oversee Vision Center promotion, maintenance, and tours.

The dark entry room of the Vision Center contained a handful of Heritage Room items, but if the old seal were there, no one saw it. And no one remembered.

And by early 2006, executive staff were dismissed or pressured to leave—for setting up shell companies to funnel money into their own bank accounts.

Maybe that seal—that memory trigger—was important. Maybe it was like repeating "Remember the Alamo" and "Remember Pearl Harbor." Or wearing a cross to remember Christ's sacrifice. Maybe we need a reminder of how others fell so we don't fall too. Maybe this book can be that reminder.

Whether it was the corporate seal or just strong leadership, the years I served at the Home Mission Board were years of relative financial integrity. Leaders weren't perfect, but they watched the budget with reasonable scrutiny.

Appearances

Just a month after I began work, a staff photographer, my boss, and I traveled to Arizona to cover the work of some of our missionaries. As we stood in the long line at the car rental agency, our hopes of getting the car we'd reserved seemed bleak. Sure enough, when our turn came, the lady behind the counter shook her head. No midsized cars remained.

Then she brightened as she handed my boss, Dan, the paperwork for a luxury car. After the crowded plane, I was pleased at the thought of a roomy Cadillac or Buick for the next few days.

But Dan shook his head.

"You don't understand," said the harried woman. "There's no extra charge. It's a free upgrade."

"Sorry," said Dan. "We'll wait for a midsized car."

As we dragged our luggage to a metal bench to start the long wait, Dan explained, "It all has to do with the green memo." John, the photographer, laughed knowingly.

"That's how we refer to a memo that just happened to be printed on green paper," Dan continued. "Larry Lewis [HMB president] reminded us that we should avoid all appearances of impropriety. An example was taking a free car rental upgrade.

Even though we didn't pay for a luxury car, everyone would think we did.

"Tomorrow, we visit a Navajo reservation. Our missionary—and the people he ministers to—live simply. We can't drive up in a Cadillac."

Refusing that free upgrade spoke volumes to me. It reminded me that we were spending someone else's money, and others were watching how we spent it.

Larry Lewis, the president when I joined the HMB staff, followed the same rules he imposed on others. He cautioned us not to accept free upgrades, and I once saw him decline a limo sent to the airport to pick him up for a conference.

At the beginning of his time at HMB, Larry and his wife, Betty Jo, saved Board money by packing a lunch when they drove from Atlanta to Nashville. He drove to Birmingham to get better airfares.

But tiny changes occurred over time. Eventually, I heard, Larry insisted on a spacious hotel suite at the annual denominational meeting. And each quarter, when Broadman Press sent agency presidents an expensive supply of sample books, he turned them in at the HMB bookstore and got a donation receipt for taxes.

Good examples

I wasn't at HMB long before I started hearing stories of the "old-timers" and how rigid they'd been with approving expenditures. Past president Arthur Rutledge once refused to approve a reimbursement for renting a U-Haul to carry supplies to a Florida conference.

"How many cars did you take?" he asked his staff. When they acknowledged that several had driven their personal vehicles, he shook his head. "Then you could have packed the conference supplies in your back seats and trunks. Sorry. No approval."

And I soon realized we had a living legend still working in the Executive Office. Dr. Ernest Kelley was a vice president who was known for his financial integrity. Once, in a meeting where people were considering what he felt to be extravagant expenditures, he called a break. When the meeting resumed, he was holding a woman's handkerchief, tied around a couple of coins.

"Don't forget," said Dr. Kelley, "that the money given to this agency doesn't come from a few million-dollar donations. It's thousands of small sacrificial gifts just like this one."

Dr. Kelley eventually became my friend and mentor. He once told me about a tough budget meeting where he and other leaders were having difficulty filling all the financial requests. He began doodling, drawing smiley faces inside the zeros in the seven- and eight-digit numbers. Suddenly, he was looking at a row of faces, and he had the answer. The budget distribution had nothing to do with who made the best presentation or who'd been with the agency longest. It was all about people: the people who gave their sacrificial gifts and the people who needed the hope only Jesus can provide. From that moment, the budget simply became a plan for distributing God's money to create the greatest blessings for givers and receivers.

Dr. Kelley said that one of his strongest reminders about the love and sacrifice behind each gift to HMB was when he was asked to meet with a group of Girls in Action.[15] The girls and their leader stopped by the HMB building to personally deliver the money they'd raised for missions: $14.

"Please do something important with this," the girls said.

Dr. Kelley struggled with how to spend this small sacrificial gift, finally putting it toward producing a children's book that was distributed to Native American children.

"These children needed to see how their money was used," said Dr. Kelley. "And I wanted it to be meaningful to them. I thought they'd enjoy knowing it went to provide a certain number of books for other children."

---

[15] A Southern Baptist girls group that studies about missionaries and puts what they learn into practice.

Cruises and condoms

Even with strong leaders like these, some people tried to operate on their own agendas. HMB accounting staff told stories of ridiculous requests for reimbursement, from receipts for condoms to Alaskan cruises. But accounting had the support of the executive office to decline payments when they felt expenses were inappropriate.

Once, under Arthur Rutledge's presidency, a new staffer turned in a receipt for a massage. When questioned about the expense, he explained, "There was a line on the expense form for 'entertainment,' and that was the way I relaxed after a hard day of travel."

The wise president said he would honor the naïve staff member's expense account one time only. However, later that day a memo went out to all HMB employees from Dr. Rutledge. He said that, as of that morning, all expense reports in the entire building had been picked up and destroyed. New forms would be available soon. And never again would HMB expense forms include the standard "entertainment" category.

Favors for leaders

Spending was conservative. Except, of course, in the case of top leaders. Once I heard from an accounting friend that during a year when staff were told there would be no raises, the HMB vice presidents quietly voted raises for themselves. I guess they'd been too busy to visit the Heritage Room.

For as long as I was at HMB/NAMB, vice presidents had inappropriate power. They were given unlimited freedom, as if somehow wisdom were attached to the title. No one could question a VP except the president. And presidents were busy people.

A new VP came to HMB, and he brought with him his dreams of publishing. Soon Darrell and his vice presidential title attracted Broadman Press, the denomination's publisher. He published *Total Church Life*, a potpourri of thoughts about church life. Knowing Broadman's high standards, I couldn't help wondering if the book would have garnered a second read if not for agency courtesy and an assurance that HMB would buy a certain number of books.

Since Darrell was operating on royalties for TCL, it was obviously to his advantage to generate as much promotion as possible. He deputized the majority of his staff to promote the book. Not content to simply assign staff to hold workshops to teach the book (though that was certainly one strategy), he also approved an enormous array of TCL products to be created at HMB expense. TCL everythings began popping up, each raising awareness of the book and increasing the VP's personal royalties. TCL binders and pens? No problem. TCL tablets, paperclip holders, and balloons? Of course. TCL tablecloths and jars of honey? No kidding. Darrell's staff had no choice but to continually come up with new ways to promote TCL.

While Darrell did not make money on the actual products and workshops, they increased his book royalties. As editing director, I saw the endless array of products come through the system. There was nothing I could do except check to be sure TCL was spelled correctly and sign the product approval form.

I decided to attend a TCL workshop to see if the product was worthy of its promotion. That afternoon the story of the "Emperor's New Clothes" took on new meaning.

Darrell set up a "non-profit" corporation to sell another of his books, *People Sharing Jesus*, to HMB. I was told that HMB bought $300,000 of Darrell's books—from Darrell—for just one evangelistic effort.

So the leadership "lid" was beginning to lower for HMB. And as staff saw that vice presidents could vote themselves raises in a year when single moms and widows learned to live on salaries unadjusted for inflation ... and a VP could enlist his entire staff to promote his personal book ... they had lower standards to strive for. And an era of integrity was closing.

As HMB editing director, I had to approve all manuscripts before they were submitted to the design department. But "approve" was sometimes a word I had to use loosely. One year in early November I received what was, to me, a disturbing manuscript. It was the story of a talking cricket telling the plan of salvation.

The drawings were crude and the story was disturbing to our materials editor and me. Carmon and I had both served on church staffs as children's ministers, and we were concerned about mixing a fictional character with the truth of the gospel. When we read the cricket's statement "Sometimes I just don't feel saved," we shook our heads in disgust. Somehow a cricket discussing his salvation seemed irreverent to say the least.

The booklet was written by Richard, a friend of Bob Reccord's who later became a NAMB VP. I expressed our concerns to Richard and another evangelism director, Thomas. They sent me a formal memo stating that not only had a children's minister approved the copy (Thomas' wife was a children's minister) but also the children's workers of Woman's Missionary Union (who wrote the SBC girls mission materials) approved—even praised—the copy.

I reluctantly approved the manuscript. Later the design director said he'd had to stop by HMB on his day off to sign an approval to pay the artist who, according to Richard, "needed the money quickly." The design director said the amount Richard requested was higher than HMB's standard payment.

A few months later, a friend at WMU called me about another matter.

"I'm disappointed that WMU approved the booklet about the cricket," I spoke candidly.

"Mary, oh no!" she exclaimed. "Do you mean to say you printed that? We did NOT approve that manuscript. We thought it was horrible. We begged evangelism staff not to move forward with that booklet. In fact, we sent them a memo pleading with them to reconsider."

"Can you fax me that memo?" I asked.

I took the memo to Wayne, my boss. He was furious and promised to show it to our executive vice president, Bob Banks. "I'll be traveling with Bob next week, and I'll put it in my folder of topics to discuss."

When Wayne and Bob returned from their trip, I immediately asked how Bob had responded.

"He just shrugged," said Wayne.

Fresh start

In 1995, the Southern Baptist Convention approved a restructuring called "A Covenant for a New Century" and implemented it in 1997. The committee that conducted the restructure study looked at ways to consolidate work that had been duplicated and to develop a plan that would make better use of contributors' money.

The study showed that some SBC agencies could close their doors and their work could be absorbed by other agencies. And it showed that the work of the Home Mission Board, Brotherhood Commission (Memphis), and Radio and Television Commission (Fort Worth) could be combined. In June 1997, these three agencies combined to form the North American Mission Board, which would operate out of the new HMB facilities in Alpharetta, Georgia.

Conservatives were elated. Merging the three agencies meant eliminating numerous positions. It was the perfect time to clean house of those pesky liberals who'd slipped in over the years.

The climate was changing. The house needed cleaning. But how do you furnish a clean house?

Jesus warned us in Matthew 12:43-45 that if we remove an unclean spirit and don't fill the empty space with something good, the unclean spirit will return and bring other unclean spirits with him, making the last state worst than the first.[16]

---

[16] Matthew 12:43-45 (KJV): When the unclean spirit is gone out of a man, he walketh through dry places, seeking rest, and findeth none. Then he saith, I will return into my house from whence I came out; and when he is come,

Conservatives were removing their problems, but they were leaving room for an infestation of misuse and entitlement. We were getting ready for NAMB.

he findeth it empty, swept, and garnished. Then goeth he, and taketh with himself seven other spirits more wicked than himself, and they enter in and dwell there: and the last state of that man is worse than the first.

Section 3   Where We Are Today

Chapter 5
Lobster in the Pot

We had two years to prepare for consolidating three agencies. During the final months before NAMB was formed, HMB leaders did their best to prepare us for the human resource massacre they knew was approaching. Periodic emails from the executive office reminded us that the new agency would be smaller. All of us would not have jobs, but the changes were designed to save money and make us more efficient.

Most of us chose to believe we'd be one of the fortunate ones who would not only have a job but would rise quickly in the new organization. We lived in a state of denial until April 1, 1997, when the first calls came. Support staff were summoned to human resources and either given a job in the new agency or dismissed. Management-level staff received letters offering them positions. No letter, no position.

Red flags

Rumors spread about who would be president of the new agency. Rick Warren's name surfaced, and he publicly stated that he had declined. Bob Reccord's name surfaced next. I heard that Bob was making almost-daily calls to his friend Richard. Bob had worked briefly at HMB about 20 years earlier and he knew Richard from those days. Richard was my peer. We were both department directors, two levels below vice president.

In mid May, Ernest Kelley called me to his office. As director of the editing department, I was also the editor for the executive office and Dr. Kelley was interim president. He handed me a small stack of confidential resumes and asked me to edit them to a consistent length, add photos, and format them for the SBC annual meeting in June.

"These are the resumes of our new executive leadership team," he told me. "Bob Reccord will be NAMB's first president."

While that announcement wasn't a surprise, it did raise my first red flag for NAMB. For the past two years, Bob had been chairman of the Implementation Task Force, whose assignment was to carry out the plans in "A Covenant for a New Century," including merging the three agencies to form NAMB. And he'd allowed himself to be nominated for president?

I sifted through the resumes. Dr. Kelley would be a VP—great choice and a tremendous relief. Whatever else happened, we had one strong man onboard. I laughed as I held up his "resume" between my index finger and thumb.

"This is it?" I teased. It was the short biographical sketch that HMB deputation services wrote for each staff member. The deputation staff sent these bios ahead when we had speaking engagements.

"Mary, I've been here so long I haven't needed anything else." That was Dr. Kelley's excuse, but I chalked it up to a very small ego.

The next resume was six pages long.

"OK," I chided Dr. Kelley. "Making these a consistent length will be more difficult than you implied."

The resume belonged to Richard, my fellow department director. The one Bob called daily, and the one who wrote the cricket booklet. Such a big jump for a friend was another red flag.

"Who's this?" I asked as I flipped through a slick four-page resume, complete with color photo.

"Nate Adams," said Dr. Kelley. "He's coming from *Christianity Today*, and he's supposed to be a real golden boy." I later heard that Nate became the highest-paid VP.

I took the remainder of the resumes back to my office, closed the door, and began editing, pushing the red flags to the back of my mind and telling myself that it was a new and brighter day for Southern Baptists. I had no intention of putting a damper on "A Covenant for a New Century." It was created to save Southern Baptists money, and I believed it was created with good and honest intentions.

June 1997. An air of excitement and optimism accompanied the formation of the North American Mission Board. It was a new day filled with promise. We'd watched with heartache as scores of friends and coworkers were called in, dismissed, and left carrying boxes, photos, and potted plants. But that nightmare was now over, and we understood that the staff reductions were necessary if we were to operate with efficiency. Jobs that had been duplicated at two, even three, of the agencies were now consolidated. We were lean, and we were ready to serve Southern Baptists.

Hope and a future

One of the first bits of gossip about our new president was that he'd abolished executive parking places. At HMB, the executive office staff, though out of town as often as in, had reserved parking. I remember once looking out my window and watching a very pregnant lady with swollen ankles, dressed in a maternity business suit and jogging shoes, carrying a briefcase and waddling from the back of the parking lot. As she passed the many empty reserved parking places, I commented to someone that she should ask for reserved parking for the next few weeks. The person said she had asked and her request had been denied.

So here was Bob, parking at the back of the lot and striding confidently into the building. The VPs seemed to like the walk a little less, but it looked like Bob was enjoying leveling the employee playing field.

And he truly seemed to enjoy people. I invited him to meet some of our mission education writers a few months after he arrived at NAMB. I was surprised when he showed up—I doubted Larry Lewis would have. I remember an older writer grabbing his hands when he reached out to shake hers. Now she had the president's attention, and she wasn't giving it up quickly.

As she gripped his hands and talked longer than necessary, Bob kept an earnest gaze, nodding and smiling and making no effort to pull away. It was as if that lady were the only person in the world at that moment. Eventually, we had to tap his shoulder and physically pull him away to attend a photo shoot.

    I liked Bob, and I was glad he was our president. I had more contact with him than I'd ever had with Larry. And when he talked with me, I got the feeling that he wanted to "cleanse the temple" and start some new and exciting strategies. I sensed that he didn't like procrastination and that he liked to move quickly and confidently. And though it was to my advantage at the time, I sensed that he didn't bother going through the ranks. He simply picked up the phone and talked to whomever he pleased, without including the person's up-line supervisors.

    Few women in leadership survived the transition to NAMB, so I soon became a token woman when one was needed. I was asked to lead a half hour of the first Spiritual Focus Day. I was assigned the role of Christmas party chairperson. I was asked to serve on the presidential inauguration committee.

Leaders who can't spend

    Jack, former president of the Radio and Television Commission and later NAMB's special assistant to the president, chaired the inauguration committee. Before my assignment to the committee, I thought only presidents of the United States were inaugurated. My tax dollars pay for those events, and now I realized that my Cooperative Program dollars would be paying for Bob's inauguration.

    The two things that stand out for me from the inauguration: One, when Jack was asked by a committee member about the budget, he said there was no set budget and that everything should be topnotch. Two, the night of the inauguration was the first time I'd seen an ice sculpture at a denominational event. (It would not be the last.) I never knew whether the ice sculpture was donated or purchased at an extravagant price. It didn't matter. I kept remembering the free car rental upgrade Dan turned down so there would be no appearance of extravagance.

Leaders who can't lead

I tried to push my slight misgivings aside and focus on the positive. Nate was my new VP, and I was, for the first year of NAMB, children's strategist on the mission education team. I didn't report directly to Nate during that first year, so my opinions were based mostly on rumors. He was supervising nearly 100 people and I'd heard that he'd told one of NAMB's leaders that the part of his work he'd liked least at *Christianity Today* was managing people.

When the first marketing director retired at the end of 1997, I sent Dr. Kelley an email expressing my interest in the position, since marketing was part of his group. He called immediately and said he'd be glad to consider me for the position, but it looked as though marketing would be moved from his business group to Nate's media and mission education group.

"Nate's written a proposal to move marketing to his group," said Dr. Kelley. "He's a professional writer, so I'm sure he'll do an elegant job of persuading Bob." What about the smiley faces in the zeros? It wasn't supposed to be about who did the best job of presenting. It was supposed to be about people.

But Nate did win, and marketing was assigned to his group. In January 1998, I sent Nate an email, expressing my interest in the position. I soon learned that Nate seemed to struggle in two areas: managing people and making decisions. He interviewed me immediately but it was October before I was offered the position.

When I was promoted to marketing director, Nate became my direct supervisor, and I became NAMB's first woman director. I loved the work, but I immediately saw that Nate's indecisiveness was costing NAMB untold money. Everyone knew that his office was filled with tall stacks of papers containing requests from his directors and plans or proposals that needed to be approved or declined. I, like the other directors, existed in a sort of suspended animation, always waiting for Nate's approval on multiple projects. The magazine was ready to go to the printer, but Nate still hadn't read it and wouldn't allow it to be printed without his tedious edit of every page. Ads were booked but the unapproved copy was sandwiched somewhere in some stack. Brochures, study books, everything came to a halt as Nate struggled to keep absolute control of every printed word.

Finding it a little more endearing than the directors who waited for answers, Nate's administrative assistant suggested one year that, as a joke about his own stacks, we surprise Nate on his birthday by all bringing big stacks of used paper to a meeting.

But all these delays cost time and money. And while Nate never seemed to get to the bottom of his stacks, he, like the other VPs, struggled to gain more staff and pull more work units under his supervision.

Fierce competition

The struggle among the VPs was obvious within a month after NAMB began. Everyone was new, so everyone felt he had to prove himself. And no one was setting VP boundaries. The message was clear: If you were a VP, you were omnipotent. If you were not a VP, you were incompetent. Decisions were made at the highest level possible. And as VPs were paid six-figure salaries to edit copy and choose the background color of magazine pages, the entire NAMB system slowed to a crawl. Stacks grew taller, VPs worked harder, and those in Nate's group waited. And waited. And hoped that one day soon our stack would be chosen, we'd have answers, and we could move forward with our work.

But that never happened while I was at NAMB. On one occasion, when I was rushing to open the bookstore to coincide with the opening of the Vision Center and the annual Southern Baptist Convention meeting in Atlanta, I found a company that was able to meet our unreasonable deadlines and furnish the bookstore within two weeks. Understandably, they wanted a portion of their money upfront. And understandably, no one could make such a monumental decision except a VP.

I had to wait my turn to get a meeting with Nate. I gave him background on the company, including recommendations I'd received. I told him we needed to request the check that day in order to meet our deadlines. When I handed him the check request and supporting material, he placed it on a tall stack of papers, stood, and walked toward the door.

"I'm heading out of town," he said as he left. "I'll read all this on the plane."

We missed our deadline, and I had to renegotiate with the company. By the time the bookstore opened the following month, they were soured on NAMB. The morning of the grand opening, they called and said they were "unable to complete the set-up," which had been part of the agreement. The Vision Center grand opening was that night. Most NAMB staff were involved in the annual SBC meeting. Everyone was overbooked. I canceled all my plans and shelved books and set up displays alone, barely finishing in time to greet hundreds of guests.

Money for messes

No one seemed to be minding the store. Or the budget. The NAMB VPs were spending like children whose rich, busy parents gave money instead of time. And each year, the NAMB children pushed the envelope farther and farther.

The errors in the editorial and design unit were monumental. The first year, that unit's budget paid for all novelty and promotional items, and they had no budget limitations. The overworked staff made numerous mistakes, which were tossed as the projects were simply resubmitted.

During my first week in marketing I found a five-figure overspend on an order and asked Nate about it, showing him that the correct calculations were clearly listed on the back of the order form. He questioned the exhausted print buyer, who shook her head and replied, "I've been here six months and this is the first time I even knew there was a back to the form."

NAMB was like a handful of puzzle pieces, tossed in the air and falling quickly. We were looking for someone to put the pieces in logical order. But the VPs were involved in minutia. Most of the experienced staff had been terminated. And the president was busy with mega-church pastors, media interviews, and writing books.

Gallup Polling Data on Southern Baptists:

The proportion of Americans who identify themselves as Southern Baptists has declined steadily and significantly over the past 10 years, from 10% in 1993 to just 6% in 2001.[17]

Does anyone notice that the lobster is boiling?

Average cost of an ice sculpture: $400

Cost to provide 80 Gideon Bibles: $400

---

[17] Gallup Poll study of Southern Baptists During the same 10-year period, other Protestant denominations remained stable. "Other Baptists" accounted for 10% of Americans in 1992 and also in 2001. Methodists accounted for 10% of Americans 1992 and 9% in 2001. The number of Presbyterians remained between 3% and 5% during the 10-year period. Episcopalians stayed at 2% during the time period, Lutherans stayed between 6% and 7%, and Pentecostals increased from 1% to 3%. From http://www.adherents.com/largecom/com-sbc.html.

Chapter 6
Hollywood Bob

The financial climate at NAMB began changing, and the changes were so subtle that we were truly like the lobster placed in a pot of cold water. When the heat's turned on the change is so gradual that he cooks without realizing it.

I don't remember when I first realized that NAMB was becoming irresponsible and extravagant with contributors' money. The realization came as small dots of careless spending. And slowly I connected the dots and began drawing a picture of leaders who lived with a spirit of entitlement.

Here are a few of the dots I remember.

Image was everything

Marketing had some strong relationships with the city of Alpharetta, where our headquarters was housed, and I received communication from the executive office that "Dr. Reccord wants to meet the mayor." When I asked for clarification, one of Bob's assistants suggested I invite the mayor, and perhaps the city council, to lunch.

The cafeteria staff provided instructions for a proper lunch for Bob. Soon after NAMB was formed, Bob had locked the small conference room off the cafeteria, labeling it the Executive Dining Room. It was now used primarily for Bob and the VPs. I was to have the lunch in the Executive Dining Room, and I was to hire professional servers.

Now I have to interject that I'm a careful shopper, and hiring a professional serving staff was out of the question. One year for my birthday, my friends jokingly created covers I could use when I was ready to write my autobiography. One friend created a cover with the title "Seventy Percent Off the Lowest Marked Price," saying that my life story would have to include tales of my great bargain shopping. My NAMB expense reports listed so many meals at McDonalds that my staff once decorated my office in a McDonalds theme as a welcome home from a long trip.

I told the cafeteria supervisor that my staff and I could serve the meal for Bob and the local celebrities. She suggested that at least I use "Dr. Reccord's regular server."

The day of the lunch, the server—hired from outside NAMB—arrived in starched formal attire and curtly instructed the marketing staff on how Bob liked his meals served. The professional server would serve first, and the marketing staff would follow his lead.

Our local politicians arrived on time, but Bob was elusive that early afternoon. When our guests tired of chatting with the marketing staff, I slipped from the room and made a series of calls, trying to locate Bob. At least 15 minutes late, he walked briskly into the room, hurriedly shaking hands and apologizing for his busy schedule.

Bob's waiter led in serving the meal. Starting with the salad, the waiter served Bob first and then our guests. The waiter brought in a small bowl of Bob's special raspberry vinaigrette dressing, applied exactly the amount Bob required, and turned to take the dressing back to the kitchen.

I stopped him and quickly asked, "Would anyone else like raspberry vinaigrette?" Our guests reached for the bowls of standard dressing on the table and served themselves, insisting that was the dressing they wanted.

Bob left as quickly as he'd entered. He never thanked us for arranging the lunch, and neither did his staff. The next day I called Bob's office to ask what budget number to use for the lunch charges.

"Oh, we don't have money in our budget for the lunch," said his assistant. "Can you pay for it?"

Money meant nothing

Dot Two: Part of the plan when NAMB was formed was that we enter into a product fulfillment agreement with LifeWay, Southern Baptist's print-resource agency. The rationale was that consolidating the distribution of products would save Southern Baptists money. I joined marketing a year into the agreement, and I entered a disaster.

My team, who had worked in marketing at HMB, realized the seriousness of the situation, but in the spirit of NAMB's micromanagement, they had little input into the agreement. NAMB marketing didn't negotiate with LifeWay's marketing. Nate negotiated with LifeWay marketing, and NAMB marketing was along for the ride.

Each year the situation grew worse. NAMB was overcharged and underserved. At one point, LifeWay found a pallet of magazines that inadvertently had not been obsoleted. LifeWay hadn't noticed the magazines, so obviously they'd been no trouble. But once they were discovered, LifeWay charged NAMB thousands of dollars in storage and then charged to obsolete them.

The marketing team calculated that we could save a high six figures per year by choosing another fulfillment service. We not only studied the feasibility of getting out of the LifeWay agreement, but Rick, our marketing strategist, also located an excellent fulfillment center just a few miles from NAMB. Rick worked extra hours to send out requests for bids and analyze the bids as they came in. The local fulfillment was superior in every way.

We presented a plan that could save Southern Baptists mega money. Nate did not respond. When I had a chance to express my frustrations to our executive VP, Randy laughed as he affirmed that Nate didn't make decisions easily. But since VPs were allowed to function as omnipotent, we stayed in the agreement several more years, until Nate was able to get onboard. During that time, the money we wasted would have put scores of missionaries on the field.

Dot three: Early into NAMB, the evangelism staff created a strategy called Family to Family, and the media team produced a video to promote the strategy, including interviews with recording artist Steve Green. Since Larry Lewis had not been involved in minutia, the media staff hadn't thought to get Bob's step-by-step approval.

Our media crew was top notch, and I'd never seen them produce anything but excellent work. When they were satisfied with the video, they showed it to Bob. Bob watched a portion and then said flatly, "It doesn't pop. Start over." It was the start of something we saw regularly: The expertise and experience of scores of trained and talented people were ignored, and the preference of the president or one of the VPs was honored.

When the media staff told Bob that starting over on the video would be costly, he simply said, "Don't worry about the cost."

All about Bob

Major Dot: NAMB's culture plummeted when Bob became an author. He used the magazine editor as his ghostwriter, and since they both worked at NAMB it became more and more difficult to keep the lines clear between personal and NAMB business. Staff observed that Carolyn conferred extensively with Bob during working hours, but the more she worked for him the more vocal he became in telling the staff that he did his writing in the wee hours of the morning. The more books he produced, the more staff heard about his early morning writing.

Bob had one book published in 1987, and I assume with the demanding schedule of a mega-church pastor, that was all he had time to write. Or perhaps, like Darrell, our HMB VP, Bob's new position opened doors that would otherwise be closed to him as an author. Whatever the reason, at NAMB, he became a prolific author.

By 2000, he'd written *Forged by Fire*, and he brought stacks of his book to a meeting of directors and VPs. Each of us received an autographed copy. The book was about growth through adversity and he'd inscribed mine: "Mary, Guard your heart and I'll see you at the finish line! Bob Prov. 4:23"[18]

By 2002, he wrote a book with John Maxwell. In 2003, he wrote the January Bible Study for LifeWay. In 2004, he and executive vice president Randy Singer wrote a book. And in 2005, he wrote three more, one with Andy Pettitte and Mark Tabb, another with Randy, and one with his wife, Cheryl. He and Cheryl also opened a for-profit ministry called Total Life Impact, Inc.[19] Bob, along with Cheryl, was listed as an available speaker and Bob's books were heavily advertised on the website. When the February 2006 article in Georgia's *Christian Index* questioned a variety of Bob's management and financial decisions, most of his photos were quickly removed from the site and he was no longer listed as a speaker.

Bob not only had ample time to write more and more books and speak at more and more non-SBC events (including an agreement to speak 19 Fridays—more than a third of the year's Fridays—at Promise Keepers rallies in his last days at NAMB), he now, like HMB's Darrell, had a staff to promote his books.

One afternoon, Michael Cooley called and asked if I could stop by his office to talk about marketing. Michael worked in Bob's office. The first thing he asked when I entered his office was, "Can you put Bob's new book in the NAMB catalog?"

I said, "Absolutely not. It's not a NAMB product."

Though Michael said he understood, he was obviously frustrated.

"Well, can you help me with some marketing for the book?" Again, my answer was no. I was paid by Southern Baptists to promote NAMB products.

He shook his head and sighed. "I don't know what to do. Bob's driving me crazy. He calls me at 10 o'clock at night, talking about promotion for his book. Basically, my whole job now is promoting Bob's books."

---

[18] "Keep thy heart with all diligence; for out of it are the issues of life."
[19] Per information on file with the Georgia Secretary of State.

I knew Bob was focusing hard on his books. I'd heard staff say they'd seen stacks of his books in the NAMB shipping center and wondered who was paying for the books and who was paying to ship them.

As more books were released, Bob's promotional needs increased. Even after I'd resigned, I was asked by our media staff to stop by to film an interview for a video an outside publisher was producing to accompany one of Bob's new books. At least four NAMB staff were involved in planning and filming the video during NAMB working hours.

Bob's obsession with gaining a reputation for being more than NAMB's president eventually resulted in NAMB paying $12,000/month to outside PR firms, even though he had NAMB's public relations team at his disposal. And though these PR firms could improve his image outside NAMB, the consensus inside seemed to be that Bob was too busy writing books about leadership, integrity, and "steering clear of the dangers that could leave you shipwrecked"[20] to address these issues in his own life and career.

Though Bob's salary far exceeded the salary of the last HMB president, he branched out to books and for-profit speaking ministries.

More and more, Bob seemed to enjoy the good life. He illustrated a point in chapel by describing a recent snorkeling trip. His biographical sketch on the Promise Keepers website described him as "an avid scuba diver, hunter, golfer and reader. This past summer he paraglided off of the Swiss Alps."[21]

His books, media appearances, company car, $12,000-a-month public relations bill, and exotic hobbies gained him the nickname Hollywood Bob. As those on NAMB's lower echelon heard stories of chatting with the U.S. President, accompanying the evangelism VP (along with their spouses) to a chaplaincy meeting in Europe, snorkeling, and paragliding, eliminating

---

[20] Subtitle for *Beneath the Surface* by Bob Reccord, with Foreword by John Maxwell.
[21] www.promisekeepers.org/conbios, March 2006 data.

executive parking places no longer seemed like an impressive gesture. His lifestyle surpassed that of other NAMB staff, and we knew it surpassed that of most of the people giving sacrificially to NAMB and through the Cooperative Program.

Cost of one month's outside PR work for NAMB: $12,000

Cost to send 24 children to school for a year in Tanzania: $12,000

Chapter 7
Six Cents Worth of Butter

It seemed that Bob liked to speak and write more than manage an agency. Google his name and you'll find blurbs for his books, promotions for his speaking engagements, and an occasional quote. If you search long enough, you'll find this story attributed to him.

Do what I say

"Dr. Bob Reccord tells of an experience he learned about while in the business world. A major institution that ranked among the Fortune 500 was working to make an unheard-of move. They were going to promote a thirty-eight-year-old vice president to president.

"The man was an impressive businessman who wooed and awed the board of directors. Upon completing the final interview process, the board broke for lunch, with plans to offer this man the prestigious position of president after they all returned from lunch. This young man went to lunch alone at a cafeteria, but was unintentionally followed by several of the board members, who stood in line behind him.

"When the young man came to the bread section, he placed two three-cent butters on his tray and covered them up with his napkin. As he checked out he never revealed the hidden six cents' worth of butter.

"When everyone returned to the boardroom for what was to be a joyous occasion, the mood had dramatically changed. The promising young man was not only denied the helm of the company but was fired from his position as vice president--all because of six cents' worth of butter."[22]

When news of NAMB's investigation reached the media, 41 denominational leaders (primarily mega pastors) rallied behind Bob. What he'd done, according to them was simply make "mistakes of the head, not the heart – the kinds of misjudgments that innovative leaders make in an effort to accomplish things that have never been done before."[23] In spite of this small flutter of support, Bob's own words convict him.

Bob implied in his story that any dishonesty was too much, that a man who cheated a cafeteria out of six cents deserved to be terminated.

Not what I do

But as a trustee audit revealed numerous incidences of irresponsible spending, from thousands to millions, Bob publicly expressed no embarrassment. When trustees reportedly instructed his wife to return $2,000 to NAMB, he did not publicly apologize or acknowledge guilt. And he clung to his job as the bad press dragged NAMB down with him.

When Bob finally resigned, according to NAMB staff, he showed no remorse. He did not apologize and instead talked about the many successes NAMB experienced while he was president, even though he wasn't directly connected with most of them. He turned his bad press into a compliment by proclaiming that he was just too "entrepreneurial" for denominational work.[24]

---

[22] From Leighton Ford Evangelism Leadership Seminar, 1991, quoted in McHenry's Quips and Quotes, cited in the computer software program for *Stories for Preachers and Teachers*. Also quoted on LifeWay's Proclaim Online as a sermon illustration: www.lifeway.com/proclaim.

[23] "Reccord supporters release statement about NAMB work and leader's integrity," www.churchcentral.com, April 21, 2006. See Appendix 4 for statement.

[24] See Appendix 2 for the full resignation and trustee chairman Barry Holcomb's response.

Till someone spoke

The extravagance that non-VP staff were helpless to change... incidences of misuse that most former employees signed a legal document promising not to report ... dishonesty that staff heard whispered but were paralyzed to address ... much of this was brought into the open by the article in the *Christian Index*. Finally, someone had the courage to speak.

Managing editor Joe Westbury, assisted by editor Gerald Harris, published the well-researched and well-documented study of the first nine years of NAMB's existence. The article[25] raised a number of crucial questions about whether forming NAMB had made the SBC's work more efficient and more cost-effective. The article left the average reader questioning whether NAMB and its leaders were a wise choice for Southern Baptists. But chief among the issues of concern were those related to Bob.

The article told of campaigns and events designed to bring money to NAMB, which instead resulted in huge financial losses.[26] It described the Vision Center, which cost a minimum of $1 million to build—and another million to disassemble and reallocate the space. It told of an alarming drop in NAMB's strategic reserve funds—from $55 million to $23 million.[27]

It described numerous speaking engagements at non-SBC events, including the 19 Fridays at Promise Keeper rallies.

The article brought to light the relationship between Bob Reccord and Steve Sanford, a relationship NAMB staff had observed in helpless silence. It told how Steve had been paid to conduct a NAMB audit, then paid to carry out the plans in the

---

[25] See Appendix 3 for entire article.
[26] One conference, Elevate, was planned to generate revenue. Instead, it lost more than $.6 million its first year. Yet two more Elevate conferences were scheduled for the next year.
[27] Trustees later reported that the starting strategic reserves were approximately $51 million instead of $55 million.

audit.[28] And it revealed that Bob and his wife had formed Total Life Impact, a for-profit corporation that promoted their books and offered their speaking services.

Applying the brakes

Trustees immediately appointed an eight-member committee to audit NAMB's finances—which revealed more misuse of funds.[29] They called a special meeting to discuss their findings, which they presented in a 19-page report. The meeting resulted in placing strong controls on Bob's leadership, including:[30]

1) "directing the travel, speaking, and on-campus office time required for the President...."
2) "the use of RFP's (Request For Proposals), akin to bidding to compete for work being outsourced by NAMB."
3) "when the President ... wants to develop new initiatives, including the appropriate oversight and approval by the Board."
4) "clarifying what constitutes poor management by an executive officer and how it should be handled."
5) providing Reccord and NAMB "with greater levels of accountability to the Board and the Southern Baptist Convention."
6) Under the sixth part of the plan, the board assigned "its duly elected officers, in perpetuity, with the role

---

[28] The trustees conducted their own audit after the *Index* article was released. They found that Steve had received $3.3 million from NAMB, for everything from private jets to running ad campaigns.
[29] Including Bob's use of two outside public relations firms, totaling $12,000 per month, without trustees' knowledge and while having a full public relations staff available at NAMB. The trustee audit also discovered what they described as a "top down" management style and a "culture of fear" among staff.
[30] Trustee response to *Christian Index* article, published on www.namb.net.

of monitoring these controls, utilizing them as part of the President's annual review, and reporting the status of these controls annually at an assigned full Board meeting."

The day before the trustee meeting, COO Chuck Allen and two of his staff, Benj Smith and Rick Forbes, resigned and/or were dismissed. The *Index* article raised the first questions about Chuck's and his assistants' conflicts of interest. Next Level Leadership was developed and produced at NAMB. LeaderShop was an outside entity under which Chuck Allen and Benj Smith published and sold materials with an uncanny resemblance to Next Level Leadership materials. Ironically, with Chuck and Benj attempting to extend their work beyond their duties at NAMB, the LeaderShop materials promised to help the participant in "obtaining true contentment regardless of your present situation."[31]

Word spread that auditors also found invoices to a third entity, LeaderShip, which led to Rick Forbes quick exit.

Sunday best

What had happened to the system of checks and balances that should have prevented Bob from having his godlike power in the first place? In my opinion, it was a matter of size and mind-set.

As a director, I attended trustee committee meetings, and there was little room for trustees to ask tough questions. Even more serious, there was no way for them to know what the tough questions were.

The trustees were divided into committees, with one committee for each VP's work assignment. Each committee elected a chairperson who presided over its meetings. But the content for the meetings, at least in Nate's group—the meetings I attended—was provided by the VP.

---

[31] http://www.leadershop.com/featured_book.html, May 31, 2006.

Before each trustee meeting, Nate told his directors to send his administrative assistant short summaries of their teams' work. Glenda compiled the team summaries and placed the written report in the trustee folders. Then Nate chose two or three directors to give oral reports at the committee meetings.

The written and oral reports were our Sunday best. We smiled and told them about our wonderful work. The trustees smiled back, assuming that everything was as wonderful as our reports. I remember only one instance of our committee questioning any aspect of our work.[32] The next month, the director in question presented a polished and positive report to answer the trustees' concerns. And everything was rosy again.

Nate prepared a report for the committee chairman to present to the full committee. This larger group of nearly 60 trustees knew nothing about a particular VP's work except what was presented in the committee's report. And questions arose only when a committee chairperson made a recommendation that required full-board approval.

At HMB, the trustee's budget report was half an inch thick. Sometimes the detail seemed overwhelming, but you could find anything you needed to know. At NAMB, the trustee budget was reduced to a handful of pages and listed only large general categories.

So NAMB sat like a patient in a hospital gown, with its back to the wall. All NAMB was showing the trustees was its front side and it seemed impolite to ask them to turn around.

And as long as leaders weren't showing their backsides, why should others? The more we heard rumors like the one of Bob attempting to submit a bill to accounting for his "donation" to NAMB's Christmas toy drive,[33] the more we noticed questionable behavior with other staff.

---

[32] A trustee asked why NAMB used non-Southern Baptist student missionaries.
[33] Thanks to strong leaders in accounting, charges like this were refused.

The Bob virus

Nate told me he decided not to write if he couldn't be paid personally. He said in 1999 that executive VP Randy Singer had ruled that if you wrote about subjects that were your NAMB assignment, they should be considered a "work made for hire" and you shouldn't receive royalties. When Bob's books blurred these lines, other NAMB authors surfaced.

Ed was in the church planting area, and he had two church planting books published by Broadman & Holman.[34] The issue of the flagship magazine that came out the same week as the *Index* story included a full-page B&H ad for Ed's church planting books. Ed was paid for his outside writing. He used Carolyn (who also ghostwrote for Bob) to write revisions for one of his books, stating that he'd probably end up paying her his whole fee from B&H.

Eric served in church planting, too, and he wrote a church planting book with Ed. I remember one day, before I left NAMB, hearing him chatting casually about the royalty percentages he and Ed were getting for their book. It was all open and accepted. I didn't blame Ed or Eric. I doubt they were aware of Randy's earlier ruling and I didn't know if the rule was still valid. Bob's books may have changed the rules.

No big deal for big wheels

The trustee audit showed that NAMB paid $3,772.64 for Bob and Cheryl to fly to England for the premiere of *The Chronicles of Narnia* movie. It showed $12,000 per month for outside PR firms to promote Bob, whose goal was to appear on CNN, even though he also had an internal public relations staff.

---

[34] Two more were released with other Church Planting staff, plus Ed had his fifth and sixth books due for release in May 2006 (from www.newchurches.com).

Bob seemed unashamed of these findings. Maybe these just weren't big enough issues to worry about. Maybe the six cents worth of butter was just a Hollywood Bob story.

Soon after Bob resigned, 41 SBC leaders issued a statement of affirmation for Bob, expressing total support.[35] Some signatures were noticeably missing—NAMB executive staff, SBC agency heads. Only one college president and three state executives signed. But those who did sign sent an alarming message. Their signatures said that a couple thousand dollars to attend a movie in England was no big deal, and if Bob wanted to direct $3.3 million in business to a friend without requests for bids, his status made that behavior acceptable. These mega pastors seemed to be in complete agreement with Bob's behavior, and their signatures made a grave statement about the management style of mega pastors.

The virus spreads

Lack of financial integrity reaches far beyond dollars, and NAMB showed this lack in intangible ways, too. I was once called into a meeting where an outside advertising/PR firm presented a detailed plan for promoting volunteer missions, the flagship magazine, and mission education. Nate asked the company to make changes and resubmit the proposal until they'd eventually spent more than 100 hours on the project.

At that point, it was Nate's prerogative to turn down the proposal, which he did. However, about a year later, I mentioned the proposal to an editor in mission education, and she said she was familiar with it.

"Nate gave us the proposal and said to use it as a go-by for developing our own plan."

Another intangible way that NAMB operated with less than financial integrity was in lowering the salary structures for staff. When NAMB was formed, those who were offered positions were given a starting salary and shown a salary range

---

[35] See Appendix 4 for full letter and a list of those who signed it.

for the position. Most of us were low on the range and were encouraged that we had plenty of room to grow.

Less than two years into NAMB, the HR director called a meeting of team leaders and told us casually that the salary structures were being lowered. Though actual salaries weren't cut, some staff now found themselves at the top of the scale with no room to grow. They could no longer receive raises. At best, in good years, they received bonuses in lieu of raises, but no money was paid into annuity (retirement) on bonuses. While millions were thrown into pet projects, the majority of NAMB operated on a shoestring.

Million dollar slush fund

When trustees dug deeper into the budget, following the *Index* story, word spread that they discovered that Bob had a $1 million fund he could use at his discretion, no questions asked and no receipts required. Each year, that fund was replenished. In Bob's last two years as president, the fund was reduced to $350,000. In keeping with Bob's operating policy, many trustees were unaware that the fund existed.

A reasonable person would have to wonder what kind of financial reporting was going on that made it possible to hide $1 million from trustees.

It's simply too easy to hide money in a big organization.

Trustees eventually deemed the slush fund "exorbitant" and reduced it to $50,000, with requirements that the new president itemize spending from the account.

"Monumental fibbing" and "exceedingly fanciful" claims

In 2003, NAMB's media arm—FamilyNet—became entangled in a lawsuit between Sky Angel and EchoStar Communications (d.b.a. Dish Network). The claim was made that NAMB/FamilyNet misrepresented themselves as non-Christian programming in order to gain access to Dish Network, which had an exclusive contract with Sky Angel for Christian programming.

The case was heard by U.S. District Judge John Kane, and reported in *Christianity Today*: "Kane ridiculed [NAMB] claims that FamilyNet isn't religious programming, and suggested that both the Southern Baptist network and EchoStar were dishonest. 'To describe FamilyNet as anything other than Christian-religious programming is absurd,' he [Kane] said. 'By analogy, one would have to say that Leonardo da Vinci's "The Last Supper" is not a religious painting because it merely portrays thirteen men having dinner.'"

The article stated that prior to FamilyNet joining Dish Network, it had been part of Sky Angel. In 1998, FamilyNet signed a contract with Sky Angel in which they certified that they were predominantly Christian programming and acknowledging that they were aware that Sky Angel had an exclusive contract with EchoStar/Dish.[36]

But when FamilyNet decided to go with Dish, they stated that they were not primarily Christian programming. *Christianity Today* quoted Kane as saying "There was no evidence adduced at the hearing even suggesting that FamilyNet has endured a programmatic epiphany. The only inference is that in presenting itself to EchoStar, FamilyNet engaged in some monumental fibbing."

Evidence provided at the trial showed that FamilyNet, represented by Randy Singer, Bob Reccord, and former FamilyNet president David Clark, had gone to extraordinary lengths to redefine to Dish Network many well-known Christian programs as more secular than Christian, listing such shows as *The 700 Club, The Call, Cherub Wings, Faithprints, Gateway to Truth* (a Bible study led by New Orleans seminary), *Time for Hope,* and *Truth Quest* as "educational" and *Gaither Homecoming Hour* and *Gospel Jubilee* as simply "entertainment."[37]

---

[36] "Christian networks battle over Dish Network," ChristianityToday.com, July 15, 2003, http://www.christianitytoday.com/global/printer.html.
[37] From the January-March 2003 programming classifications provided to Judge Kane by FamilyNet. This programming classification was an attachment to a January 23, 2003, memo from David Clark to Eric Sahl, "RE: Responses to Letter."

In correspondence to Dish Network, provided as evidence at the trial, David Clark stated that these programs, if religious at all, simply referenced a "higher power" and that if these programs were included as religious, "many programs on television such as *Oprah, Dr. Phil,* and many others in day time secular television would be [sic] have to be considered 'religious.'"[38]

Randy Singer, who served as NAMB's legal counsel, seemed to walk a lukewarm line by stating in a *Baptist Press* article that FamilyNet's programming was evangelistic rather than religious, as defined by the Dish Network contract with Sky Angel, which uses the phrase "solely marketed to the Christian theme and content."[39]

Randy quickly cried First Amendment violation, stating that if Dish Network ordered FamilyNet off the air "solely because we're Christian,"[40] they would be violating the First Amendment and he prayed that wouldn't happen. How does that match with his earlier claim that FamilyNet was not solely Christian? If they were taken off the air for being Christian, then they were Christian. And if they were Christian, they violated the exclusive contract Sky Angel had with Dish.

Judge Kane saw it the same way. When the constitutional concerns were raised at the trial, he called Randy's claims "exceedingly fanciful" and said they did "not merit further comments."[41] Eventually, an arbitration panel ruled unanimously in favor of Dominion/Sky Angel and awarded $2.43 million in damages and $748,000 in legal fees.[42] Of this, NAMB paid $600,000 in contributor dollars.

According to a source familiar with the lawsuit, "Sky Angel would have let it go with just an apology if Bob Reccord hadn't been so arrogant throughout the entire situation."

---

[38] January 23, 2003, memo from David Clark to Eric Sahl "RE: Responses to Letter."
[39] Ibid.
[40] Ibid.
[41] Ibid.
[42] quoted on www.satelliteguy.us.

Cost for Bob and Cheryl to fly to England for the premiere of *The Chronicles of Narnia* movie: $3,771.64

Cost to send a layperson on a two-week mission trip to Honduras: $2,000.00

Chapter 8
Friends in High Places

It paid, quite literally, to be Bob's friend. And if you couldn't be a friend of Bob's (sometimes referred to as an FOB), it was second best to be friends of one of the VPs. Sometimes the lines of all those friendships blurred.

FOBs

Bob promoted long-time friend and cricket booklet writer Richard to VP even before he was officially elected president. Within months, Bob also brought John Yarbrough, another Implementation Task Force member, on board as evangelism VP. John had stepped up to chairman of the ITF when Bob stepped down so he (Bob) could be considered for president. So two of the 10-member task force that organized NAMB, and both its chairmen, landed six-figure NAMB positions.

Bob also brought a half dozen or so members of his Norfolk church with him to NAMB. They performed at a variety of competence levels. But when he brought his old friend Mike Carlisle, cronyism took on an even more dismal meaning.

Not long after I became marketing director, Tom asked to meet with me. Sounding more like a used car salesman than a church planting manager, Tom tossed around numbers like $40 million as he told about a software system they'd just purchased: Church Planting Management System (CPMS). Staff members usually overestimated success of their products, hoping I'd put more marketing effort behind them. But even the most enthusiastic originators seldom talked in millions.

I heard from several sources that Mike Carlisle was paid $100,000 for the CPMS software, which he'd developed before coming to NAMB. I was told he was paid quickly so he'd receive the money before moving to Alpharetta. That way he wouldn't have to count CPMS as a "work made for hire," which would mean his salary would be considered his payment.

The stuff kings are made of

Mike came to NAMB as director of our computer area, but from the start, he acted as if he were on a higher level than other directors, and certainly his spacious, plush office confirmed that he was destined for greatness.

Mike reminded me of a bipolar bumper car. He'd ask me to stop by his office, where he'd spend 30 manic minutes talking promotion for CPMS and other computer and Internet issues. Then months would pass without his mentioning the ideas again.

After purchasing CPMS and then (I heard) spending an additional six figures developing it, NAMB learned that LifeWay already had a similar product and had for some time. They ended up giving CPMS away. It became one of many products and events projected to generate income that ended up costing contributors' dollars.

Mike had many other big plans, but nothing seemed to develop into a successful product or process. When NAMB was going through yet-another restructure, rumors spread that Mike would be VP of a newly formed group. One curious director asked Chuck, the chief operating officer, to lunch so he could find out if Mike would be his (and my) VP. This director asked specifically if Mike would be a VP, and Chuck responded quickly and emphatically, "Never. Mike has failed at everything he's done at NAMB, and he'll never be a VP."

The next week, Mike's new business cards went through the editorial and design system. His title? Vice president. Maybe it would have been appropriate to add FOB below his title.

I'd struggled with Nate, and I told myself over and over that if I could just get out from under what I considered Nate's micromanagement and indecisive leadership, things would be fine. When Mike became VP, I had to face the reality that NAMB didn't have a Nate problem. It had an executive leadership problem, and it started at the top. I now felt that most of Nate's problems were from leadership immaturity and lack of supervision. I resigned within a month after moving to Mike's group.

Girls should be girls

On a Friday afternoon in March 2004, Chuck asked to meet with Mike and me. In his usual direct and unemotional way, he casually stated, "Mary, I think you're a competent and talented leader. Trouble is, two vice presidents don't like you—Nate and John. It's your work on the PPAM that's angered them."

Randy, our executive VP, had earlier assigned me to chair a Priced Product Approval Matrix to try to get control of some of NAMB's ego-driven products. Until the PPAM, a VP could produce virtually any book, novelty item, or brochure he wanted. As long as he had the budget, his omnipotence was honored. The PPAM, with representation from each area—including financial, now had to approve all products, and we used marketing analyses to guide our decisions. All of a sudden profitability won over egos. This was demeaning to NAMB royalty and though I only voted to break a tie, the VPs blamed me personally when one of their products was declined.

"So here's what I need you to do," said Chuck casually. "Just keep being the strong businesswoman you are. But I need you to be sweet and feminine to John and Nate. That way we can keep these guys happy."

My husband, Jack, picked me up about an hour later. I told him about the meeting and he simply said, "God gave you leadership skills and intelligence, and I believe He planned for you to use them. I want you to quit. God will take care of us." So on Sunday I emailed my resignation, effective in two weeks. And God did take care of us. I had just turned 55 in January, and I learned on Monday that I was eligible to take early retirement.

Who pays for silence?

I followed the rules in leaving and in taking retirement. I got exactly what was paid into annuity. I didn't ask for a special deal, and I was offered none. But NAMB had a way of adjusting retirement benefits for special friends or people they simply wanted to leave quickly or quietly. An employee had to be at least 55 and have 10 years of service to retire. Though one VP was only 50 when he left, his age was adjusted to make it possible for him to "retire." The magazine editor's years of tenure were adjusted so she could retire. Special deals abounded. With those special deals came increased financial benefits, and someone ultimately paid these additional benefit costs. And since NAMB was supported by the SBC Cooperative Program, sacrificial gifts ultimately paid for additional benefits.

But with special deals came restrictions. Nearly everyone who left during the transition to NAMB and afterward was required to sign a letter promising not to speak or write about NAMB. The letter included these restrictions and penalties:[43]

"In consideration of the enhanced separation benefits that the North American Mission Board of the Southern Baptist Convention, Inc. (hereinafter collectively "NAMB") offered to me ...

"I covenant and agree that all monies received under this Agreement will become immediately due and payable to NAMB if I should ... breach any term of this Agreement ...

"I further agree to ... make no statement or to take any action which would result in any publicity or disclosure concerning this Agreement. Additionally, I agree to keep confidential all aspects of my employment relationship with NAMB, except for disclosures compelled by legal process and agree not to divulge or use any confidential information obtained in the course of my employment with NAMB to the detriment of NAMB. I further agree to make no public or private statements or disclosures concerning my employment or treatment by NAMB

---

[43] See Appendix 5 for the entire document.

or any of its officers, directors, or employees, and not to portray them in a negative or poor light to anyone."

Because I left willingly and under positive circumstances, not asking for or receiving an enhanced benefits package, I was not asked to sign a copy of this "Release and Waiver Agreement."

Former staff were unable to speak. Current staff knew that, to keep their jobs, they couldn't question or complain. In this climate of forced silence, Chuck was able to tell one group of employees that if they didn't like the direction the bus was going, they should get off the bus. I heard that he told another group that if they didn't like what was going on, they could use any of the 16 building exits.

As one blogger, an anonymous NAMB employee, wrote after the publication of the *Index* exposé and the resulting NAMB trustee audit: "I am a man who prides himself in his willingness and even eagerness to say what needs to be said in the open light of truth and honesty, secure in God's promise that 'The truth will set you free.' The problem is that the only thing that the truth will set anyone free from inside the walls of NAMB is gainful employment. Granted, the fact that Chuck Allen (who roamed the halls like an officer in the KGB showing anyone who disagreed with him one of the sixteen exits to the building) is gone does indeed remove a great deal of tension from the building.

"But until 'Hollywood' is gone, all the assuredness from the Trustees in the world can't protect the 'unwashed mere mortals' from retribution from this guy who literally does wander the halls pondering who the Judas is that 'did this to him' like some sick remake of Nixon in the final days."[44]

---

[44] From www.misfityouthworker.blogspot.com/2006/04/well-i-asked-for-feedback-on-namb.html.

The half dozen

It's been said that the SBC is run by a group of about 35 people.[45] NAMB was run by a half dozen.

In the months before I left NAMB, the staff watched helplessly as these half dozen leaders—Chuck, Randy, Mike, John, Richard, and Bob (though Bob was usually a member in absentia) made plans for yet another restructure.

As plans formulated for this latest reconfiguration, the word was that marketing would move to the newly formed group. Mike Carlisle invited me to half-day weekly meetings, officially to deal with the audit conducted recently by Steve Sanford, an outside consultant who—like Randy and others in Bob's inner circle—just happened to be a member of Bob's former church in Norfolk. Steve and Mike co-led the meetings.

To me, it became clear quite early that one purpose of the meetings was to form a strategy to pull as many work units from Nate as possible, making the new group plump and desirable.

And it became clear that Mike did not care for Nate. On one occasion, I arrived for the meeting a few minutes early to find Mike in a tirade about Nate. Steve coached him calmly, telling him to bide his time, that everything was going to move smoothly and it would all be over soon.

It would have seemed surprising that Mike and Steve could be so confident in implementing all their ideas if it hadn't been for what Mike had told me about his relationship with Bob. Seemingly oblivious to the implications of what he was saying, Mike told me he'd worked with Bob years ago, and they'd gone their separate ways. Then he received a call from Bob saying the program he led at HMB was being eliminated and he was looking for a job. Mike was able to find Bob a position at Evangelism Explosion, where he worked.

---

[45] April 1, 2006, article in the Lakeland, Florida, *Ledger,* by religion editor Cary McMullen.

Friendly fire

Mike sent me an email one day asking for a recommendation for product fulfillment for a friend of his, Kendall. It was at the end of a string of chatty emails between the two friends, which ended with a "by the way, do you know a fulfillment house" from Kendall.

In next week's strategy meeting, Mike presented some possible companies we could use for an elaborate new Internet system that would bring in millions in sales of priced products (income which was never realized). One company, Kintera, was not cheapest, but we were told that over the course of several years it would be most cost effective. We were polled individually, and one by one everyone voted for Kintera. I'd had no background in this extensive study so I voted with the rest. A few weeks later I learned that Kendall would be hired as a consultant, along with his assistant, Maria, to oversee the transition to Kintera. Before Mike began as VP, he called together his million-dollar consulting staff to carry out his work. The consultants made it much easier for Mike to schedule a new fence for his backyard and a couple of days' dental work during his first week in his new VP position.[46]

Mike started with a staff of 40-50 in May 2004. By May 2006, he was down to 5, with many of his employees let go and the work outsourced to InovaOne. InovaOne Studios, Inc., was owned by Steve Sanford and incorporated at his home address on December 1, 2004, just in time to receive the lion's share of NAMB's outsourcing in 2005. He also registered three limited liability companies the same day: InovaOne Aviation, LLC; InovaOne Enterprises, LLC; and InovaOne Strategies, LLC.[47]

---

[46] I personally tried to locate Mike the week he was elected as VP, and his administrative assistant gave me these reasons for his absence. The election occurred during At Home Week, a week designated each month for all staff to be in their offices so meetings could be conducted. To be out of the office during At Home Week required a VP's approval.

[47] Per information on file with the Georgia Secretary of State.

Immediately after 28 NAMB staff were terminated in the fall of 2005, I received emails from friends asking, "Have you seen the InovaOne website? It looks like NAMB is their only customer." I checked out the site and found three full-page endorsements: one by Bob, one by Randy, and one by Chuck. Though I found a few minor jobs that Steve had apparently completed at some time in the past, it appeared that InovaOne was definitely held together by NAMB dollars.

A later audit by trustees confirmed that NAMB paid InovaOne for a variety of tasks, including:

> InovaOne's media strategies audit: $35,000
>
> InovaOne's consulting contract for implementing the recommendations he'd made in the audit: $300,000
>
> Outsourcing media: $745,000
>
> InovaOne video: $1,700,000
>
> InovaOne private airline hours (through Airshares): $142,374

The trustees initiated the audit after the Georgia Baptist state paper, *The Christian Index*, ran a story on February 16, 2006, called "North America: Hanging in the Balance."[48] Steve immediately attacked Joe Westbury, the article's writer, on the front page of his InovaOne website calling the story tabloid journalism.[49]

After reading the story, I checked the rest of the site. The NAMB endorsements were gone. I could only assume that Joe's story worried NAMB's inner circle and their friends. It was highly unusual for anyone to question their actions and they were apparently uncomfortable with this new level of scrutiny.

---

[48] See Appendix 4 for complete article.
[49] See Appendix 6 for complete web article.

After Bob resigned in April 2006, NAMB attempted to get out of the multiple contracts Bob and Chuck signed with Sanford and InovaOne. Trustees learned that some were for as long as three years and, as one person described them, the contracts had "no wiggle room." NAMB finally spent more than a million more dollars of contributors' money to buy out just one of the InovaOne contracts—contracts most trustees had known nothing about.

Though Nate seemed to be outside the inner circle, he was a VP. And with that title came a certain degree of perceived omnipotence. Not long into my career in marketing, I had a fairly successful day and reported some impressive strides to Nate via email, along with an expression of how much I enjoyed my new position. He'd seen, even in mission education, that I would stand up (OK, dig in my heels) for what I believed to be right or fair, and we'd already disagreed about a number of things. He answered my emailed success report with: "We're going to get along fine as long as you don't chafe against what I want."

At least in his dealings with me, Nate found room for only his opinion. And his opinions cost contributors plenty. Three incidents come immediately to mind. The third was the first step in my deciding to leave NAMB.

Phantom consultant

At budget time, Nate called another director, Mike, and me to his office. We were told to bring our budgets. Mike was director of publishing and responsible for the agency's flagship magazine.

"I've got a consultant I want you to use—Roy Coffman. Roy was my boss at *Christianity Today* before he retired, and he's a real go-getter. He knows marketing, and he can get sales up for the magazine and all our products. We'll have to pay him quite a bit, but [the song that became NAMB's theme] he'll bring in lots more money than we pay him."

Mike and I were told to open our budgets. Nate had already located four separate budget items, two in Mike's budget and two in mine, where we would pay Roy.

"We'll take $1500 out of each of these budgets," explained Nate. "And you can share Roy's time." Fifteen hundred times four budgets times 12 months equaled $72,000 a year. It was more than I was making as marketing director, so I hoped Nate was right about Roy.

I saw Roy a total of three times in a little over a year. From my perspective, he served NAMB as a ROAD (Retired On Active Duty) warrior. Working seemed the last thing on Roy's mind. He enjoyed telling "Nate stories": how close his family was to Nate's, how he never gave Nate a real performance review—just took him to lunch at Chili's and said "good job this year" as they were leaving, how Nate had been the young "mascot" VP at *Christianity Today,* keeping a bowl of candy on his desk and planning Christmas party skits. Maybe it was worth a few dollars to see this picture of Nate, to understand why he had difficulty managing and making decisions—but $72,000?

I told Nate my concerns about Roy.

"You're not being clear on what you want," he replied. "You need to tell him what you need. Give him a catalog and tell him you need some products promoted."

The next time I met with Roy, we sat across from each other at a small table in my office. I was armed with the catalog. I pushed it across the table and suggested that he help us promote some products. Roy maintained eye contact as he slid the catalog back toward me and replied, "Trouble is, I don't know any of your products."

He got up. "I need to be going. Can your secretary call me a shuttle to the airport?" He walked to the door, then turned back. "Oh, yeah. And who's going to pay for my shuttle? Should I just have them send you a bill?"

My frustrations mounted with Roy, so one day I asked Mike how he was faring with Roy's marketing. "If he's spending a lot of time on the magazine," I told Mike, "I guess I can understand his not having time for my work."

"I figured he was spending his time with you," said Mike, "because he's not doing anything for the magazine except selling ads. And he gets paid extra for that."

I voiced my concerns about Nate's friend Roy to anyone who would listen. No one did. Eventually, I understand, Nate and Roy had a falling out and dissolved the agreement.

Dollars and sense

As leader of the PPAM, I had a second and separate budget outside marketing and outside the control of any VP. This seemed a constant annoyance to Nate. After all, how could anyone who wasn't a VP make a financial decision? VP decisions plummeted NAMB into financial distress, but seeing a tiny budget item he couldn't control seemed unbearable for Nate.

When Randy called me into a budget meeting when Nate was out of town, he offered me $100,000 to promote priced products. His rationale was that a marketing staff could come up with promotion that would increase sales better than the array of novelty items[50] VPs usually approved. I was elated until he said he'd put the $100,000 in my marketing budget instead of the PPAM's. I'd seen Nate juggle my budget before, once moving all the existing general marketing money to an account to be used only for his group and telling me that now that he'd contributed marketing money for his products, the other VPs would have to do the same. Before I realized, I blurted out, "Then I'll never see the money."

"If you don't get the money, you let me know," said Randy.

When Nate and I met about my budget, the money wasn't there. I asked, "Where's the $100,000 Randy gave me to promote priced products?"

"The money was put in my budget," said Nate. "And I've already distributed it among the other teams."

---

[50] Standard novelty items included mugs, computer cleaning brushes, hats, and golf shirts all bearing the names of NAMB programs and strategies. Some NAMB staff wore free golf shirts the majority of their work days.

One of my team members later told Randy that we didn't get the money. He shook his head helplessly. No one was putting parameters on NAMB royalty. And somehow $100,000 that could have been used to promote products, getting important messages into the hands of believers and bringing income back to NAMB, was "distributed among the other teams."

No peace in troubled times

But nothing was as upsetting as the $5,000.
The Iraqi war had just begun, and Randy challenged each team to think of a way they could respond quickly to the crisis. My team had a retreat at a team member's house on a Friday and I asked them to brainstorm something marketing could do. The team suggested that we compile a book for military personnel and their families with stories by well-known people who had been through difficult times.
The book seemed like a monumental task, considering our workload, but the enthusiasm was high. I suggested that we pray about the project over the weekend, and anyone who was still interested come to work a half hour early on Monday and we'd discuss it.
Not expecting as much enthusiasm on Monday as Friday, I arrived the half hour early and was the last of my staff to arrive. My administrative assistant had brought coffee for everyone and we gathered in my office—around the little table, against the wall, on the floor—and used a dry marker board to compose a list of possible contributors. Then we divided the list and each person promised to make contacts. Since I was the only one with writing experience, I agreed to write the book, primarily at night and on weekends. The book would belong to NAMB and none of us would put our names on it.
It was one of the most enjoyable projects I was involved in at NAMB. We placed a bell in a central area to ring each time a well-known person agreed to be part of the book. Halfway through a day, I'd hear the bell ring and then a shout: "Rick

Warren said yes!" Then later, "We've got Chuck Colson" or "Janet Parshall's onboard!"

I met with Nate to tell him about the book, but he disliked the idea immediately. He didn't stop us from writing it but he wouldn't support it. He'd written several books and was an excellent writer, but he was the only VP who didn't contribute a story. True, for Bob and most others, I had to write the stories or do monumental editing on some warmed-over sermon, but they participated.

The PPAM approved the book. An outside print buyer found a great printing deal and the PPAM approved using them. So the book made money, which was a rare accomplishment for a NAMB product. By the time the book went out of print, it had sold 20,000 copies—with only $5,000 to promote it.

I worked long hours, seven days a week, with my team sending me everything from faxed sermons to whole books they'd gotten permission to use to create our short stories. In less than three weeks, the book was at the printer, and it was a powerful collection of stories and encouragements called *Know Peace in Troubled Times*. I wrote the foreword under Bob's name, and no name appeared for the author/compiler. For one of the few times in several years, the marketing staff felt that they'd done something worthy, and it was uplifting.

But we had no money to promote the book. Nothing. And with my promotion budget all moved to a budget item specified for Nate's projects, there was nothing I could draw from for even a small ad.

My husband, Jack, and I inherited a substantial amount of money early in 2003. As we wrote tithe checks, we had what we felt was an exciting idea. Why not put a few thousand toward the promotion of *Know Peace*? It was a win-win plan. People could read the stories of comfort and encouragement and selling some extra books would actually bring money back to NAMB.

"But I want to give the money anonymously," I told Jack. "I want to keep it low key."

Low key turned out to be impossible.

The next day I sent an email to Carlos, our CFO and a contributor to *Know Peace*, and asked how I could handle an anonymous gift to marketing for promoting *Know Peace*. Carlos assured me that the only people who needed to know who gave the gift were Bob, Claude (the development director), and Mitch (our controller). He said he'd send an email to Mike Cogland, a member of my team who handled promotion, and tell him about the gift.

Carlos sent the following email to Mike titled "Designated gift to help promote book "Know Peace in Troubled Times": "Mike, a donor who wishes to remain anonymous has given us $5,000 for the sole purpose of promoting the above-referenced book. You will be the only person to have authority to spend these funds for the designated purpose. Please give Marilyn Taylor a call and she will give you the account number. If you have any questions besides who the donor was, please feel free to call me or come by my office. Take care. Carlos"

The phrasing of the email was Carlos' choice, but Nate took issue with his stipulation that only Mike could spend the money. I forwarded the email to Nate with the message: "FYI. Just wanted you to know, if you see some promotion out there, that we haven't redirected other promotion dollars."

I fully expected Nate to be happy that we had some promotion money that didn't affect his budget, but "Do you know who the donor was?" was Nate's sole reply.

"I believe they want to remain anonymous," was my answer.

"I understand the word anonymous. How then did you become acquainted with their identity?" Nate asked.

I could see Jack's and my gesture souring. How did I answer him without lying and without angering him further? I tried a noncommittal response: "Carlos sent me this email."

Once Nate got started on an email trail, there was no stopping him. He kept pushing: "I am inferring the fact that you know the identity of the donor because you answered my question below by saying they want to remain anonymous rather than saying yes or no. So my question remains about how you became acquainted with their identity if they asked to be anonymous."

You'd have to understand the climate of fear under which non-VP staff lived to see that my choices were now limited. I called Jack to see what he wanted to do. As a federal agent, he was used to working in an open environment where strong personalities of all levels could voice their opinions. He was adamant that Carlos had promised us that only three people besides himself needed to know. We weren't telling Nate just because he was a VP who wanted to know. The gift would lose its joy if everyone knew who gave it.

I sent Nate's string of emails to Carlos and asked for his advice. I labeled my email "confidential." He suggested I tell Nate. Still communicating on an email trail labeled "confidential," I replied: "I just called my husband and he said absolutely not. Nate may guess that it's us, but he doesn't know for sure. Would I be expected to tell who the donor was if it were someone else? I'm unclear as to why Nate, above anyone else, should know who gave an anonymous gift.

"When I asked about giving the money, I was promised that only you, Mitch, Claude and Dr. Reccord needed to know, and that was the agreement under which we gave it. Jack said that if Nate insists on knowing, we'd like our money back.

"I know you're only suggesting that I tell Nate, but you're sensing that telling him is the only way to stop his questioning. An employee should not be harassed by their boss to provide confidential information. Nate's emails are inappropriate.

"I appreciate being able to confide my frustrations. This has turned from a joyful expression of support for the book to a stressful situation. We will soon inherit significantly more money, and we no longer feel we can give it anonymously through NAMB."

Carlos had been a friend for a long time. He saw the "confidential" on the email, and he never discouraged the email conversation, which went well beyond what I've quoted here. But a few days later I received an email that showed me with chilling clarity that VPs had no boundaries.

The email was from Carlos, but I had a strong feeling that he was assisted in writing it and that somehow my confidential email to him had been read by Nate, with or without Carlos' approval. He told me that since he was an officer of NAMB it was his responsibility to report the contents of my emails to HR because I had accused Nate of harassment and that Nate and Mike Day, the VP over HR, would be talking to me about the situation.

The meeting was held the next day. Nate had, without my permission, already been told that Jack and I were the anonymous donors, and he appeared pleased as he told me that he knew. Mike, though a VP himself, simply took notes as Nate read a long, convoluted description of my insubordinate actions and his innocence throughout the entire ordeal that he had been thrust into. As I sat in that meeting, watching and listening to Nate make incredible accusations, I knew I was powerless. I simply listened as Nate laid out the method by which the money would be spent by Mike Cogland and approved by him as VP.

I asked myself if opposing Nate was worth losing a job I felt God had called me to do. I decided it wasn't. If I took the money back, my team would be disappointed—they'd been thrilled that someone was supportive of the project and assumed it was one of the well-known contributors we'd included in the book. So I agreed to Nate's plan.

Marketing did everything right. Mike made careful plans to spend the money, saying more than once that he felt responsible for using the money wisely. When he took the check requests to accounting, an accounting clerk made a mistake and the requests didn't go to Nate for approval. Carlos later confirmed that it was indeed an accounting error.

But Nate never asked. He simply drew the conclusion that marketing had circumvented his approval. While I was working at the annual SBC meeting, he gave Carlos instructions to return the check and not to notify me that it was being returned. Carlos, in one miniscule gesture of rebellion, refused to just have the check show up on my desk. He emailed to let me know it was being returned.

A month or so later, I saw Carlos in the hall. We were walking to the basement with a shoulder-to-shoulder crowd of employees in response to a tornado warning. I noticed Carlos beside me, avoiding eye contact. The entire ordeal had been an embarrassment to him. I took the initiative and greeted him. He seemed relieved that I wasn't angry.

"Mary, some day I'll be able to tell you everything behind what happened," Carlos told me. "It was handled badly."

With a full-time development director asking for money, even on a website where Muslims, Buddhists, and pagans asked for donations,[51] a vice president had the power to return $5,000 because he incorrectly assumed he'd been left out of the spending process.

Mike had carefully spent the $5,000 to promote *Know Peace*. When the money was returned, I still had to pay for the promotion. So I took $5,000 from an already bare budget to cover the costs—money supplied by sacrificial gifts and spent unnecessarily.

Returning the check was the beginning of my emotional detachment from NAMB. The VPs were out of control, spending more time in power struggles than leading their staffs. The president was too busy writing and speaking about effective management to realize what was happening in his own backyard.

A lid too tight

NAMB's "lid" grew lower and lower, driven by a mind-set of entitlement, and staff members with high standards were smothering. One by one, they left. On the day I told my staff I was leaving, one team member blurted out, "All the good people are leaving."

A NAMB-wide anonymous morale survey, managed by an outside company, showed that Nate's staff rated him extremely low, the lowest of all the VPs, with several people labeling him a "micromanager." He brushed off the criticisms

---

[51] NAMB was listed on http://www.networkforgood.org/topics/religion.

by rationalizing that the people in his group were more creative and therefore more emotional. NAMB staff was promised there would be improvements and that NAMB would mark progress with follow-up surveys. There were no more surveys.

Cost of returning a donor's gift for a VP's ego: $5,000.00

Cost to serve 41,667 meals to hungry people in Uganda: $5,000.04[52]

---

[52] From the Ethics and Religious Liberty Commission flier in the 2004-2005 Royal Ambassador Resource Kit, item 40b "Hunger Facts."

Chapter 9
Surpassing the Joneses, Competing with Kings

To understand Bob's mind-set, you'd have to understand the entitlement rationale of a typical large-church pastor. Bob came to NAMB from a mega-church in Norfolk, and from what I heard from church members he brought with him, Bob was loved. If he lived the same lifestyle at Norfolk that he lived at NAMB, his extravagance was either unnoticed (possible) or accepted (also possible).

Mega

A mega-church pastor may have been placed in a large position because of faithfulness and dedication (Luke 16:10), and he may be a powerful influence. But a mega-church pastor can, if he chooses, live a royal life. His only check and balance is the deacon or trustee body, and if he relates well to that group, he's home free. The budget is then virtually his.

I once served on the ministerial staff of a large-though-not-mega church. Our pastor of 20 years retired and the 13-member search committee decided we needed a younger, state-of-the-arts model. They set some standards which, to me, left the Lord's leadership out of the picture. They set an age range, an educational minimum, and even unwritten qualifications for the pastor's wife. One candidate was rejected because his wife was overweight. Another was rejected because his wife was too attractive since a certain country-club female member would "scratch her eyes out."

So right from the start, the decision was a manmade one. The pastor who accepted our offer fit the manmade requirements. And once the wheels were in motion, the committee began calling Gary "God's man for our church," and they were determined to bring him to our church, no matter what a closer look revealed.

On one of Gary's visits to our church, he slipped into the media center and read the minutes of previous church business meetings. He discovered that, a few months earlier, the committee had asked another pastor to consider our church—a man with a great deal more experience than Gary. The other pastor was offered more money, and though Gary had already accepted a financial package (Matthew 20:13), and he was coming from a tiny church and had no experience with managing any size staff, he demanded more money.

While most church members were anticipating God's man for our church, the pastor search committee and deacon body were hurriedly changing the financial package to accommodate royalty-in-training. Even though Gary was coming from a small church, he knew how to play the game.

At budget time the next year, Gary told me that a pastor who graduated from seminary with him was making $30,000 more than he was. I knew at that moment that Gary wouldn't be satisfied until his salary equaled his friend's. He'd been slowly "working" the deacon body and, sure enough, that year's budget had a new format: all salaries were lumped together and only a handful of us knew that the lion's share of the increase went to Gary. When someone at the business meeting asked for a breakdown, Gary told them they were welcome to come by the church office to see individual salaries if they "had a need," but the grouping was done to ensure privacy for staff members. The minister of education's secretary confided to me that she was paid minimum wage while Gary's salary was adjusted to match his friend's.

A "smart" large-church pastor can learn to work the deacon body until the deacons are embarrassed to question his dealings. And Bob learned early to work the trustees in the same way.

Trustee insurance

A little over a year after Bob came to NAMB, the trustees presented him with an elk statuette, about a foot high. He immediately ordered a custom-made display case, and word spread that NAMB paid $5,000 for it. He placed the display case in the main lobby so the trustees would see how much he appreciated their gift.

One tiny lamb

And what could make the trustees feel better about NAMB than a public display of evangelism? While the elk's display case was being built, the VPs came up with the idea of a rack of free tracts. Nate told me to order a nice wooden book rack to place by the main exit, designed to hold tracts and small booklets.

"And have a sign made for the top of the rack that says, 'As you leave, take one. Remember, you're on mission.'" The idea seemed like a good one, but I was unsure why Nate asked me to order the rack. Until I learned that marketing would not only order the rack, but we would also pay for it, keep it stocked, and pay for the tracts. Would we receive extra money in our budget to pay for the tracts? No money was available. We'd have to take the money from our bare-bones budget.

The tract rack, as well as the lunch for the mayor and my $36,000 share of Roy's consulting fees, illustrated to me that the entire NAMB budget belonged to the president and his VPs. If a trustee studied these leaders' individual budgets, they'd only have a partial picture of their spending habits. It was always possible for the president and VPs to dip into someone else's budget to carry out their plans. It reminded me of the prophet Nathan's illustration to King David. When David had Uriah the Hittite killed so he could marry his wife, Bathsheba, Nathan told David about a rich man with large flocks of sheep. When the rich man had a guest, he sent his servants to the poor man's house to take the poor man's one small lamb to kill and prepare for supper for his guest. Over and over, NAMB kings dined on the tiny budgets of the rest of the staff.

Micro/mega

NAMB was run much like a mega-church, where the pastor is the unquestioned leader. But it was run with a certain micromanagement that is rare in a mega-church. Most mega-church pastors have no desire to know how the preschool is run. They don't ask what's being served for Wednesday night supper, and they trust the minister of education to train the Sunday School teachers. But Bob and his VPs had a bizarre mixture of detachment and over-involvement. They had too many outside interests to have time for personal involvement, but they didn't trust the staff to make the smallest decisions.

While few of us saw Bob or talked directly with him after the first year, we felt his presence. He personally selected the chairperson for each year's staff Christmas party, but that didn't necessarily include direct communication. In 1999, I received a call from Bob's secretary, saying that Bob was asking me to serve as chairperson for the Christmas party planning committee.

"Dr. Reccord wants two serving lines this year. He wants to use the same Santa the Chick-Fil-A staff uses—I'll get you the contact information. And he wants a brass ensemble playing in the foyer as guests arrive," she told me. Fair enough. We could do these things. So I pulled together a talented committee, and we met regularly to plan.

Kay was in charge of entertainment. The year before, we'd had a choir from a local church, so this year Kay suggested we have a comedian. Kay was a super organizer and soon had a stack of tapes of local comedians. Then someone on the committee remembered Bob's level of involvement. "I guess Dr. Reccord needs to approve the comedian," I agreed reluctantly.

So Kay selected a comedian and gave Bob the tape to approve. He listened to the tape and declined. She chose another comedian, and he declined again. When she gave him the third tape, he told her, "I don't like any of these, so I've already asked Charles Billingsley to be the entertainment." Billingsley was one of Bob's favorite performers; he sang at Bob's inauguration.

The following day, Kay sent me an email stating that since Dr. Reccord was making all the decisions concerning the Christmas party entertainment, there was no need for a committee member to be in charge of the same thing. She resigned from the committee.

While the Vision Center was being built, Nate decided that the NAMB bookstore needed a facelift and should be called the On Mission Resource Center. "On mission" was a phrase Nate thought he'd brought with him to NAMB, though the SBC Woman's Missionary Union in Birmingham had had Women on Mission groups for years. Nevertheless, he named the magazine *On Mission* and declared the phrase our new and trendy slogan.

With the opening of the On Mission Resource Center coinciding with thousands of Southern Baptists converging on Atlanta for the annual convention, we planned some gift items that tourists could purchase. Of course, all expenditures had to be approved by Nate. So our six-figure VP sat at a table in my office and tediously went over the list of pencils and bookmarks.

Knowing how grandparents like to purchase T-shirts that say "future President" and such, we'd planned some infant and toddler-size T-shirts that said "Missionary in Training." Nate had three sons, ranging in age from about seven to 13. When he saw the design for the T-shirt, he pushed it aside and shook his head. "My sons wouldn't wear that." The royal word was issued. End of story.

Who pays for micromanagement?

The frustration of not being able to make decisions paralyzed most of us, but it also cost contributor dollars. What reasonable person would suggest paying someone a quarter of a million dollars a year to plan the details of a staff Christmas party or to listen to tapes of comedians? Or pay more than half that for someone to copy edit, choose magazine photos, or approve gift items for a bookstore? But that's what Southern Baptists paid for low level decisions. A chimpanzee could have done most NAMB jobs because our work was mindlessly carrying out the dreams of a small royal family.

Can trustees be trusted?

We knew the situation. The trustees did not. We wanted to tell them, but we realized that talking to the wrong person could mean that the message would be delivered directly to Bob and the VPs. And we could become one of those employees who was escorted from the building as if we'd been caught stealing. If for any reason Mike Day —the VP over human resources—felt that someone being terminated might cause a stir, they'd be escorted out by a couple of healthy-size men as the rest of us watched. Even if the person's job was simply eliminated and the departure was on friendly terms, if Mike thought the exiting employee had potential to cause trouble, the person's computer would be locked and their password changed while they were in HR being terminated. Their personal belongings would be boxed up, and they'd be escorted out the front door.[53]

So when the trustees came to town, we put on our paper doll clothes and folded the tabs back neatly. And we'd line up in the hallway with our backs to the wall, presenting our good sides. The president and VPs had built cozy relationships with the trustees, who now accepted the smiling paper dolls and would never have offended Bob by asking questions.

Marketing was encouraged at one point when our committee chairman, Will, suggested that each of Nate's trustees spend an afternoon with a different team, talking in depth with

---

[53] Nearly 100 employees were terminated or took "early retirement" during the nine years Bob was president and at least two lost their homes and are now renting apartments. At least one professional was forced to apply for Medicaid and food stamps.

them about their work and then reporting back to the other trustees. And Will specifically asked to meet with marketing.

Our team planned our time carefully. We even discussed how we'd answer if Will asked how things *really* were. But when the big day came, Will didn't ask the hard questions. He spent most of the time telling us about his small church and his raceway ministry and we soon guessed that the request to meet with marketing had nothing to do with learning more about the agency. It appeared Will had chosen marketing hoping we'd have some giveaways he could use in his work. He'd occasionally asked for free or obsolete materials in the past— even free shirts from the On Mission Resource Center.

So the trustees were no threat to the royal lifestyle, as long as Bob and his VPs knew how to work the relationships. The trustees met a few times a year, and we simply put on our Sunday best during those times. A mega-church pastor like Bob knew how to work the system, whether it were a deacon or trustee system.

Ask an expert

Ask anyone hands-on in a work environment how to improve and you'll probably get a helpful answer. Companies that involve all levels of employees in decision-making save time and money. But HMB and NAMB weren't set up to receive input from any level but the top.

I'd always felt that what HMB, and later NAMB, lacked was healthy lower-level input. I wrote a memo to the HMB executive office and later to human resources, suggesting that we form an employee council to raise issues that would improve morale, save money, and increase efficiency. No one responded to my memos. I added under "additional comments" on my NAMB morale survey that we desperately needed an employee council. It was never mentioned.

During a director/VP planning retreat, we broke into groups to brainstorm ways to improve the agency. Someone in our group suggested that we encourage bottom-up ideas, and everyone agreed. We put our suggestions in writing, but none were implemented. VPs continued to make decisions on background colors for magazine pages. The president continued to be involved in minutia. And morale plummeted as the rest of us realized that our ideas would never be used. Those who were taller than the NAMB lid moved on.

35 kings, 16 million worker bees

When the *Index* story broke in February 2006 and Bob's extravagant lifestyle was partially exposed, trustees struggled to match the *Index* story with the pretty reports we'd placed in their committee notebooks. The vote was equally divided between trustees who supported Bob and trustees who wanted him to step down. As word of this book became known, I received what was supposed to be a reassuring message. I could take heart because Paige Patterson, one of the strongest SBC leaders, was "on my side." He also wanted Bob to step down.

The article in *The Ledger* (Lakeland, Fla., newspaper) stated what most denominational workers had known for years: about 35 people ran the SBC.[54]

The SBC consisted of more than 16 million worker bees, who supplied the royal jelly for a small band of leaders. Sixteen million of us supplied the money for them to carry out their personal strategies. No more than 35 people ran the SBC, and Paige was one of them.

Paige wanted Bob to resign because, according to the person who told me not to worry, he already had "his man" ready to move in.

Paige and I had one thing in common. We both wanted Bob to resign. As a Christian, I believe every person can, by the power of God, change any behavior and mind-set. But there's a price to pay for putting material things before God, just like there's a price to pay for all sin. I hoped Bob would step down and rebuild

---

[54]The April 1, 2006, article is written by Cary McMullen, religion editor for Lakeland, Florida's *Ledger*.

his ministry in a new setting. NAMB could never again be a joyful ministry for him or for anyone under his leadership.

As a blogger said, "It could be said that the compassionate person would want to allow him a dignified way out so that he can move on and maybe go back into the pastorate. NO WAY! NOT NOW! He has not only done immeasurable damage to NAMB, but he has done serious harm to the personal lives of many good, talented, and most of all, dedicated Christian people whom he threw to the curb in only one phase of this saga of misdeeds. Are we really sure it's a good idea to allow him to just go waltzing into the pulpit of some unsuspecting church where he can be the same old egotistical headline grabbing camera hog that he is now? Do we really feel good about setting some unwary church up to be run millions of dollars into debt in some megalomaniacal drive to look 'world class'[55] (him, not the church).

"I think he should be made to start from scratch and fight for his next job through the shame of having been fired from this one, remembering that the only one whom he has to fight with is himself and his own desire for glory and accolade. Yes, yes, we all know that it is Satan who is really at work. But Satan only gets in the game if we cast aside the help that only the Lord can give us and let him in. I like the idea of helping Reccord out. But he can't be allowed to start from where he is. He must start from that same penalty box that Jim Bakker and Jimmy Swaggart (among many others) went to. Let us not forget the fate of Moses, Saul, Solomon and so on...

"It is now time for Bob to go back to boot camp and learn how to march again. But that means he has to be bounced from the rank of general all the way down to private."[56]

---

[55] Bob Reccord often told NAMB staff that everything they did must be "world class."
[56] The same articulate anonymous NAMB staff blogger in www.misfityouthworker.blogspot.com/2006/04/well-i-asked-for-feedback-on-NAMB.html.

Yes, I wanted Bob to leave. But I didn't want Paige's or any other man's choice for a new president. Paige had, according to the SBC political experts, systematically made selections for a string of key SBC positions. I didn't want to see another Paige selection at NAMB's helm. Hadn't we learned anything from Bob's careful maneuvering from ITF chairman to president? Wasn't it time to ask God who He wanted as NAMB leader? Wasn't it time we got back on task?

Million dollar dreams, 50 cent assignments

One of the saddest things about NAMB's royal spending was that crucial projects suffered to provide money for personal preference spending. While Bob was criticized for chasing projects that weren't part of NAMB's assignment, his indirect response was that he was "too entrepreneurial" for a denominational agency. But the bottom line is that if appropriate time and money had been devoted to NAMB assignments, it would have been nearly impossible to carry out unrelated assignments.

Even if the projects that lost millions for NAMB had instead been highly successful, they simply weren't NAMB's assignments. The Southern Baptist Convention makes assignments to each agency, and NAMB had many specific, expensive, and time-consuming assignments. When Bob and the VPs redirected funds, they caused SBC-assigned ministries to operate on Jenny Craig budgets.

The first time I read an Ardor Group email that criticized NAMB's indecisiveness and poor management,[57] I was struck by the amounts being tossed at a single media campaign. According to Ardor Group, NAMB originally planned an $11 million media campaign and ended with a campaign of only $360,000. $11 million was so far from any amount I'd dealt with at NAMB that I hardly noticed that figure.

---

[57] See Appendix 7 for Ardor Group email.

But spiraling down to $360,000? That was more budget than I had for an entire year to do all the promotion for NAMB products. And every year, I was one of many directors who was told to cut the budgets again, to find something else to do without, to find a cheaper way to do one more thing, even though the overall economy and contributors giving remained strong, if not robust

NAMB's questionable spending seemed, to me, to be a top down, lead-by-example mind-set. Bob's "outrageous and irresponsible spending" was a regular part of NAMB gossip.

Most of us knew that when Bob's son was married, the Reccords held the rehearsal dinner at NAMB. Cheryl called at least four NAMB staff—Steve, Bert, Mary, and Cliff—away from their assigned work to set up and decorate for the dinner.

Personal favors ranged from a few hours of lost work time to vacations masked as retreats. As director of the Priced Product Approval Matrix, I was invited once a quarter into the inner sanctum of the ELT (Executive Leadership Team) meeting to give a brief report. On one occasion, I slipped in at my assigned time and found a seat along the wall. Bob had slipped out, and when he returned he didn't notice me. He slid into the seat at the end of the table, and I was behind him.

He drew out his words with extreme satisfaction: "Wait till you see the retreat we have planned for you this time." He went on to describe a resort in Destin, Florida, where the ELT would be holding their upcoming planning retreat.

After each ELT meeting, Bob and the VPs met the directors in the auditorium for lunch. After lunch, Chuck, Randy, or some other assigned person spent hours downloading information to directors for us to download to our staffs. Bob seldom joined us for lunch and rarely stayed for the meeting, except for the occasions when he practiced his management training speeches on the directors.

But that day, Bob stayed. Since budgets were being cut once again, he explained that some might criticize the VPs for holding their retreat in a resort area.

"When we realized how tight the budget would be this

year," Bob spoke with emotion, "we tried to cancel our trip. We found that it would cost as much in penalties if we canceled the trip than if we went ahead with it. So please squelch rumors that this is a frivolous trip."

Leaking the "good" stuff

Bob liked the finer things for himself, but he seemed to love the idea of dedication and sacrifice for the staff. And he liked media coverage for our good deeds.

One of his first actions as president was to initiate Spiritual Focus Days at NAMB. He set apart three days in the fall to close NAMB and gather all staff in the auditorium for three days of prayer and fasting.

On the surface, this sounded like a great idea. But the afternoon before the first Spiritual Focus Day, we received via email a script to record on our voice mail messages. It was, in essence: "The North American Mission Board is closed for three days of prayer and fasting. Please leave a message and I'll get back to you after our Spiritual Focus Days. Please pray for us as we seek God's leadership for the North American Mission Board."

Though the acts of prayer and fasting were scriptural, the public way we announced it was contrary to how Jesus tells us to pray and fast (Matt. 6:5-7, 16-18[58]). But the days were meaningful, and we were even asked to spend time during lunch and after the meeting writing Encouragrams—notes to various

---

[58] Matthew 6:5-7 (KJV): "And when thou prayest, thou shalt not be as the hypocrites are: for they love to pray standing in the synagogues and in the corners of the streets, that they may be seen of men. Verily I say unto you, They have their reward. But thou, when thou prayest, enter into thy closet, and when thou hast shut thy door, pray to thy Father which is in secret; and thy Father which seeth in secret shall reward thee openly."

Matthew 6:16-18 (KJV): "Moreover when ye fast, be not, as the hypocrites, of a sad countenance: for they disfigure their faces, that they may appear unto men to fast. Verily I say unto you, They have their reward. But thou, when thou fastest, anoint thine head, and wash thy face; That thou appear not unto men to fast, but unto thy Father which is in secret: and thy Father, which seeth in secret, shall reward thee openly."

staff members telling them how much we appreciated what they did for the Kingdom's work. We prayer-walked through every area of NAMB. We broke into small groups and prayed. Our peers shared their insights and ideas about spiritual growth.

But each year, Spiritual Focus Days became less spiritually focused. Soon the tables stacked with water and juice for fasting were replaced by box lunches and catered meals. Big-name speakers, management training, and personality tests took the place of Bible studies and prayer times. But the days continued to be called Spiritual Focus Days, and each year we were given a promotional script to record on our voice mail and use as an automatic reply on email.

Mission trips were another highly promoted advertisement of NAMB's spirituality. Each staff member was not only allowed to take a two-week mission trip—he or she was required to do so—from the lowest level position all the way to the president.[59] Bob's mission trip was, of course, covered by the media. Lynn, who worked in public relations, was assigned to cover Bob's first mission trip for Baptist Press.

"He did nothing until the photographer arrived but stand around and talk to big-name people," said Lynn, "Then he picked up a hammer, the camera flashed, and he went back behind a building to continue his chat with friends."

Whose light is it, anyway?

Eventually Bob became bigger than NAMB. I was told by both Chuck and Nate to brand Bob Reccord, even though we were an agency before Bob and hoped to be one after Bob.

I expressed my disagreement with making Bob the focus of our branding effort. "We're different from Billy Graham or Charles Stanley," I told Nate. "These men have their own ministries. You give so their ministries can continue. Southern Baptists give so the missionary work can continue." Nate

---

[59] Mission trips eventually became optional.

shrugged. Though I know Nate agreed with me, the decision was Bob's. And Bob would be the focus, not the missionaries.

From the onset of NAMB, the focus was skewed. The North American Mission Board, like the Home Mission Board, was set up to be a missionary-sending agency. Southern Baptists gave their contributions so missionaries could do their work.[60] But that wasn't Nate's focus when he moved to Georgia in the summer of 1997.

HMB's flagship magazine had been called *MissionsUSA*. Missionary stories comprised 90 percent of its content. *MissionsUSA* was the PR publication of HMB. It was provided free to churches and denominational leaders, and it told them—through photos and stories—where their money went and why they should give.

Everyone understood Nate's desire for a fresh start and a new name for the magazine, but we soon learned that he also planned a new focus. He and Mike, his director of publishing, called focus groups to give input on the new magazine. I was invited to one of the focus groups.

Lois was in my focus group. She'd been a pillar employee at HMB, working in the public relations area. She coordinated building tours and her knowledge of Southern Baptist history and polity rivaled that of a seminary professor. Lois was adamant that the new magazine should continue focusing on our missionaries.

The group moderator doggedly extolled the need to get people involved in personal evangelism. Lois and several other group members acknowledged the need for personal evangelism but reminded the moderator that our SBC assignment was

---

[60] When the *Christian Index* article questioned NAMB's inflated missionary count of "more than 5,000," the trustee audit found that NAMB paid full salaries for only 32 national missionaries, plus their 32 spouses. Another 1,507 were partially funded by NAMB and state conventions, plus 1,223 unpaid spouses. The rest of the 5,154 count was made up of 2,358 volunteers who paid their own expenses.

missionaries and that nearly half the agency's contributions were given for support of missionaries.[61]

At the close of the meeting, the moderator summed up all the ideas: "So what I hear you saying is that we need a magazine that tells individuals how they can share their faith."

"No!" shouted Lois and others. "That's crucial, but our assignment is the missionaries. Don't leave out the missionaries."

When the first issue of *On Mission* magazine was released, it focused on personal evangelism, as did the following issues.

Missionaries faded, and Bob shined brighter. We all knew that Bob wanted to be in the limelight. But the desire for attention snowballed when Bob became a prolific author. His desire to promote his books reached even to the announcement of his resignation.

An anonymous NAMB staff member described the meeting Bob called with NAMB staff immediately after the trustees issued their 19-page audit report in response to the *Christian Index* article: "When all of this started, Bob held a 'family chat' with all of the employees of the building and said, 'When this story broke, I was drawn back to my book, "Forged By Fire"…' Many people would have been drawn to their knees. Others would have been drawn to the Word. But Bob, like Narcissus, was drawn back to his own reflection, and, like Narcissus, he was consumed in it."[62]

When Bob saw that—regardless of whether he were right or wrong—his ministry was tarnished, he remained two months with NAMB, amidst threats and pleas for his resignation. Everyone wondered why he would drag NAMB and its ministry down with him. I had my ideas, and they stemmed from a comment I'd heard a few months earlier.

---

[61] The Annie Armstrong Easter Offering for North American Missions generated nearly half its income.
[62] www.misfityouhtworker.blogspot.com/2006/04/well-i-asked-for-feedback-on-namb.html.

When NAMB eliminated 28 positions in the fall of 2005 and turned the work over to Bob's friend, Steve Sanford, someone outside NAMB asked Bob how the staff who'd lost their jobs were accepting the situation.

"In different ways," Bob reportedly said. "It all depends on their level of spiritual maturity."

FOB favors

We all knew that Bob threw big salaries to his friends. When NAMB had an opening for director of the technology team, an outside HR person was brought in to do the interviews. One of the candidates, Mike Carlisle, was Bob's good friend—the friend who'd given him a job years earlier. According to someone involved in the process, during Mike's interview, Bob and Cheryl burst into the room, hugging Mike and exclaiming how great it was to see him and how they missed their days together at Evangelism Explosion.

When Bob and Cheryl left, the disgusted interviewer continued. Refusing to be swayed by Mike's cheerleaders, she ranked the candidates according to their potential to fulfill the duties of the technology director. Mike was not at the top of the list.

Bob calmly told the HR staff that an outside firm didn't understand NAMB's special needs, that Mike was the person he wanted, and besides, he had bigger plans for Mike. And he certainly did. The man who couldn't receive outside approval for director eventually became a VP.

Final royal action

The spring trustee meeting was held May 1, 2006, after Bob's April 17 resignation. Bob asked for time during the closed-door evening session to address the group. Though unsure of what value such a meeting would have at this point, trustees allowed him time on the program.

Bob flew to Newark and used his time to warn trustees against managing a new president too closely. Then, according to an observer, he asked the trustees to get down on their knees as he led them in prayer. As the group knelt, one trustee at the front of the room noticed that Bob was still standing.

    A trustee asked Bob if he were going to kneel, too. Bob said, "No."

    One observer summed up Bob's actions as "making them submissive to the very end."

Cost of a $250,000-a-year president spending an hour planning a staff Christmas party: $133.33

Cost of a $30,000-a-year employee spending an hour planning a Christmas party:[63] $15.38

---

[63] Based on NAMB's 37.5 hour work week.

Chapter 10
Mistakes with Your Money

I'd been in Marketing for two months when I learned that, even before NAMB was formed, the evangelism staff was planning for Y2K. As far back as the 1950s, when we proclaimed "A Million More in 54," Southern Baptists have linked campaigns and catchy phrases to landmark dates, giving evangelism a series of much-needed boosts. The thought of a new millennium had the evangelism crew snorting fire.

The novelty business

In December 1998, Rick, our marketing strategist, showed me an order form produced at HMB, listing scores of Y2K products evangelism had already promised to produce.

"Have they thought that all these products will be obsolete on January 1, 2000?" I asked. Rick shook his head. He'd been in denominational marketing long enough to realize that if a staff member had the support of his VP, he needed no marketing analysis and no rationale other than that he had a "good feeling" about the product.

One of the first Y2K meetings was with Jack in January 1999. Jack produced a mailing each summer for state evangelism leaders, which included plans for a fall evangelism emphasis. The mailing included an order form for our products, so Jack was meeting to ask for Marketing money to order a witnessing bracelet to include in the mailing.

"How many bracelets will you need?" I asked.

"A million," said Jack without hesitation.

"*A million?*" Any lack of emotion from Jack was made up by me. Jack was talking about a simple leather strap and five cheap plastic beads—with each bead representing a part of the salvation plan. But a million?

Jack continued with the confidence of a man backed by a VP. "And on each bead will be a letter, reminding people to share Christ Jesus in the new millennium. The letters will be CJY2K—for Celebrate Jesus Y2K."

Though marketing had to sign off on all priced products, Jack already had Evangelism VP John Yarbrough's signature. The product approval form had a place for the VP not only to approve the product, but also to rank it 1 to 5 according to its priority to the VP's overall strategy. Everyone in the production area knew that John marked every evangelism product with the highest possible ranking. Jack was home free, so Rick and I could only do damage control.

Jack's theme for fall was "On Mission to Share Jesus," so we suggested that he put OMTSJ on the beads. At least they wouldn't be obsolete in a few months. He graciously agreed—if he had pushed for his original letters, John would have made sure he got them. With that obstacle overcome, we concentrated on the quantity.

Jack only needed a few hundred bracelets for the mailing so we asked if we could produce a small amount and then produce the others when we totaled the orders. He said that wasn't possible, that the product had to be ready to ship as soon as the orders were placed. He personally guaranteed that we'd sell a million bracelets.[64]

Jack wouldn't budge on the quantity. You'd think Marketing would set a quantity based on a marketing analysis, but Jack's analysis was John's signature and top-priority ranking. He held firm to the quantity and our hands were tied.

Rick did some calculations. We were talking in the high six figures for the bracelets. They'd be cheaper if they were packaged in lots of 100 and unassembled, and Jack agreed that

---

[64] That wasn't unusual. We even had people promise to write personal checks if they didn't sell the numbers they projected. Of course, when the products didn't sell, we witnessed a lot of long-term memory loss.

102

churches could assemble them as a congregation. Still, the best price Rick could find was about $400,000.

So NAMB paid $400,000 with no marketing analysis and no confidence from Marketing that the quantity was wise or the product was necessary (similar bracelets were already available at most Christian bookstores). But we considered it a major victory that we talked Jack out of CJY2K.

Editorial and design had disaster on top of disaster with the bracelets. The first ones to arrive couldn't be assembled. The straps were thicker than the holes in the beads. The unit manager flew across country to check the second batch. (Costs like these were never attached to a product, but they were paid by contributors' money.) When they were finally deemed usable, the order for 1 million bracelets was placed.

The bracelets were produced in China, and the editorial and design manager forgot to ask what method of shipping the company would use. When the order was later than expected, she enquired. The bracelets were literally on a slow boat from China. Their late arrival delayed Jack's mailing by a week or so, which was Evangelism's explanation for low sales.

Whatever the reason, the bracelets sold slowly. We paid years of storage for them. We repackaged some of them to try to at least get them into the hands of people who would use them to share the gospel, and after paying to have them repackaged, the bracelets sold for less than their cost to NAMB. Nevertheless, when I left NAMB four years later, we still had an ample supply of OMTSJ-that-were-almost-CJY2K bracelets. The total costs for advertising, production, repackaging, storage, and miscellaneous expenditures such as airfare and staff time skyrocketed the cost of the bracelets. The bracelets never made a profit and probably covered less than half their costs. I thought often about the money and time spent producing a simple novelty item that anyone could have produced. If those resources had been sent to the mission field or used to produce evangelistic materials that only NAMB could produce, what would have been the eternal results?

The bracelets were an example of VP power, loss of focus, poor judgment, and a series of mistakes that cost contributor money. A VP without marketing experience rated a product that could have been purchased in most Christian bookstores or made from supplies in a craft store as top priority for his group's strategy, and the effort pulled NAMB staff away from focusing on resources that filled a real need. Without intervention, evangelism would have produced the CJY2K version, which would have been outdated as soon as it was produced. Jack overestimated the quantity, and the harried editorial and design unit never dreamed there'd be a "ship" in the "shipping." And hundreds of thousands of sacrificial dollars were wasted.

Oops! There goes another money tree

"Mistakes" like this were standard procedure at NAMB. Nate saw the waste and tried to create guidelines to allow marketing to have some sort of approval based on analyses. But the VPs were in constant competition and if Nate wanted it, then John was against it. And if Nate wanted analyses on evangelism products, he certainly didn't want his own products analyzed. Since the majority of products were produced within John's and Nate's groups, the competition raged between the two VPs.

Nate had experience in marketing, but it was severely limited. When he graduated from college, he applied to be an editor at *Christianity Today*. The only position available was in the fulfillment/marketing area, so he began there with little or no marketing or business experience and worked his way up to VP of marketing.

Christianity Today produced magazines, so Nate had limited experience with other products. He applied his magazine experience to everything we did. Sometimes it was applicable, and sometimes it wasn't. But he was a VP, so all his decisions stood.

As Nate and John competed to prove that their products were successful, Nate's pulled general promotion money into a special marketing budget that could be used only for mission education products. And one of the most burdensome mission education products was the North American Mission Study.

The study had been simpler at HMB, but Nate's version was slick. The box alone for the NAMB version probably cost as much as the entire HMB study. The NAMB study never paid for itself, but each year the product and its promotion got bigger.

In 1999, a tiny portion of the study included interviews with some members of Wedgewood Baptist Church, Fort Worth, Texas, where a gunman later killed seven church members and then himself. One of the members who was killed had been interviewed in the study.

Nate instructed the mission education team to write a flier to attach to the bookstore sales display, letting shoppers know that the study included an interview with one of the murdered people. While those of us involved in producing the bookstore display suggested not capitalizing on the tragedy, Nate insisted. Many of us were secretly pleased when the extra advertising did not increase sales.

Eventually Darren, our marketing analyst, received more freedom (as a result of the PPAM) to analyze the profitability of a product and use that information to determine whether the product would be repeated the following year. So Nate began meeting regularly with Darren and others on our team, making sure the analysis was favorable for mission education. After one meeting, my team came to my office, angry and disgusted. Our process had always been to study profit and loss over the entire life of a product. Though the mission study was still drastically in the red when the previous year closed, Nate told my team not to carry over the expenses to the new year. The study began the next year showing that all sales were profit, guaranteeing approval for the next year's study.

Juggling figures was just one way the VPs put on their Sunday best. Whether it was the number of missionaries or the profit on a product, everyone was great at airbrushing wrinkles out of our processes. Meanwhile, project after project was failing.

"One in a Million" was a doomed campaign that was never allowed to die. The idea was that NAMB would create a viral email that would be so compelling that people would forward it like the jokes and cartoons that move effortlessly around the Internet. Those receiving the email were asked to register to pray for our country's spiritual needs, and I was told by Steve Sanford and Mike Carlisle in their weekly meetings that the underlying goal was to capture email addresses and eventually sell products to the people who'd agreed to pray.

John, the Evangelism VP, was determined that he'd register a million people, but the numbers stayed in the extremely low thousands. I never knew the exact amount spent on "One in a Million" over several years, but websites and html emails were designed, staff time was devoted to it, and ads showed up in a variety of publications. Marketing suggested that the email look more grassroots, but we were told that Bob wanted it to look elegant and slick. World class.

"One in a Million" was never the success John hoped it would be, and many reasons were given. But it was one of the projects that would not die, projects kept alive by egos and paid for by contributors' money.

The heart of the problem

I personally had a theory about why we had so many failures that drained our budgets and caused us each year to make even deeper budget cuts. In my opinion, NAMB did not have a financial problem. We had a spiritual problem.

We lived in an anti-Blackaby mind-set. In *Experiencing God*, Henry Blackaby warns us that our personal strategies and ministries are doomed to fail. He reminds us to find out where God is working and join Him. And most of the spending I witnessed at NAMB appeared to me to be ego-driven.

The Elevate conferences described in the *Christian Index* article were just another example of ego-driven projects.

Bob seemed to see himself as a mentor to young leaders. He once told the VPs and directors that he wanted to bring in carefully selected young people the following summer to be our interns. He wanted the directors to invite these young people to stay in our homes and to provide a topnotch mentoring program for them.

He asked for a show of hands in the room of 30-40 NAMB leaders. All in favor? Terrified hands shot up. But I couldn't bring myself to vote for such a big undertaking when my budget and staff had been cut severely. I simply didn't have time to carry out this phase of Bob's dream.

We'd just eaten lunch together and were seated at round tables. I was sitting at Bob's table. He hadn't noticed my hand down when he called for his first show of hands. But now he was asking, "All opposed?"

I raised my hand, along with four or five other terrified souls. I later heard that Bob was furious that anyone dared vote against his idea. He told someone he really didn't care what the directors thought anyway. The only consensus he wanted was from the VPs.

But Elevate was bigger than a handful of interns. It was his chance to go national in mentoring young people to be "on mission" whatever their occupations. He assigned Chuck to coordinate the Elevate conferences, and Chuck hired an outside publicity firm to produce a slick promotional campaign that included driving a repainted, gas-guzzling fire truck across several state lines, through the areas where the two conferences would be held.

Well-known, though sometimes nominal, Christians were on the speaking schedule, and Bob and Randy were up there with them. Chuck showed the Elevate promotional video in NAMB chapel and as the speakers flashed across the screen, we were surprised to see Bob listed as "author" instead of "President, North American Mission Board."

Elevate was touted as a conference that would not only pay for itself but also bring a great deal of money back to NAMB. The unspoken message that some of us felt we were receiving from Bob's office was, "Let us show you how to plan a successful conference."

The first year's conferences had a budget of $600,000, and NAMB lost even more than that. In spite of the financial drain of the first year, the agency scheduled two conferences for the next year. Both conferences were later canceled, but not before time and money were spent on more elaborate planning. In years when missionary requests were denied and NAMB staff budgets shaved, we found money for Elevate—an endeavor that, according to the trustee audit, eventually had a net loss of more than $1 million.

An organizational nightmare

Over and over, NAMB leaders stormed forward with little or no planning. We made promises to outside companies that we never kept. Public relation and advertising firms spent hundreds of hours presenting, reworking, and re-presenting proposals, only to be told that NAMB leaders had changed their focus and wouldn't need their services after all. Some left shaking their heads about NAMB's leaders. But Ardor Group, as one person described it, "fired NAMB," and explained in an email why they were too frustrated to continue working with them.

The September 13, 2004, email was addressed to Chuck, Bob, Mike Carlisle, John Yarbrough, Richard Harris, and six others, and it was from the three top leaders at the Ardor Group (a highly respected Christian marketing and media consulting agency). They kindly but firmly told NAMB they could no longer work with them on the "Now Is the Time" outreach project. For 17 months, they had attempted to work with NAMB on the project, describing themselves as "very, very patient through all the changes at NAMB. Changes in vision, mission, purpose and financial worries. Changes in leadership and constant management shuffling."

Arbor Group described the project, at the time they dissolved their contract, as "dull, stale and dead." Changes were made often and "all at the very last hour." Now NAMB was asking them to "go back for a third time and redo our estimate and reduce the creative costs again."

"We respectfully have had enough of all the changes," wrote Ardor Group. "At first it was an $11 million dollar media budget. Now it is around $360,000. ... If we might be so bold to suggest we see NAMB as an organizational nightmare. ..."

At this point, Steve Stanford and InovaOne were ready to step in. Ardor Group sent their email on September 13, 2004. Four InovaOne companies were registered on December 1, 2004,[65] and by late August 2005 the electronic media, editing, photography, and design areas began receiving notices that they were no longer needed. The majority of NAMB media work went to InovaOne.

The birth of InovaOne meant the demise of four NAMB units. It meant that nearly 30 creative communicators lost their jobs.

Soon these employees glutted the freelance market and applied for the same few full-time positions available in Christian ministry. Some lost their homes. They lowered their standards of living. They asked their parents for loans. They sought government help.

But NAMB was a nonprofit organization, so they were unable to draw unemployment. One mother wrote to the *Christian Index* about her son's situation. He was a professional staff member who was terminated to make way for InovaOne. His wife was seven months pregnant with their second child at the time he was terminated. This mother wrote: "Their only source of outside assistance has been food stamps and Medicaid. While they are very appreciative and thankful for this help, it breaks my heart."

This lady stated that her son had received three months' severance. It took a significant portion of the severance to pay COBRA premiums to cover the baby's birth. She observed: "I understand from media reports that Dr. Reccord possibly

---

[65] InovaOne Aviation LLC, InovaOne Enterprises, LLC, InovaOne Strategies LLC, and InovaOne Studios, Inc. Steve Stanford was listed as the registered agent for all four corporations.

received severance in the amount of two years' salary. If this is true, it deeply disturbs my husband and I as lifelong Southern Baptists, especially in light of what happened to our son and many other dedicated former employees of NAMB."[66]

Cost of a million bracelets that churches could have purchased from other sources: $.4 million

Cost of feeding 400,000 starving people soup for a month: **$.4 million**[67]

---

[66] "Don't forget those terminated at NAMB," Letters to the Editor, *Christian Index*, May 25, 2006.
[67] From the Ethics and Religious Liberty Commission flier provided for 2004-2005 Royal Ambassador Resource Kit, item 40b "Hunger Facts."

Chapter 11
Condoms and Cruises

Trustees found that only 32 North American missionary families were fully funded by the North American Mission Board. Most missionaries were somehow finding a way to preach the gospel without total support from the $126 million NAMB budget.

While Bob Reccord took $2,771.64 junkets to London for movie premieres and threw $3.3 million in business to friends, one Idaho church staffer described his work this way: "I happen to serve a church in Idaho … I receive no funds from NAMB, our state convention or anyone else for that matter. Other than a couple hundred a month housing plus 8 bucks an hour to clean the church, I'm out here on my own dime. I scrub toilets at the middle school at night so I can serve out here."[68]

My husband, Jack, and I have a deep love for the work out west and sometimes give directly to the Utah-Idaho Southern Baptist Convention. We lived in Denver in the 1970s and saw the sacrifice many pastors and missionaries made so they could serve in these areas. While we were there, one Colorado pastor had to humble himself to ask the associational office for help because he had nothing to feed his family but the lettuce he'd grown in his garden.

If the money we give to North American missions isn't reaching these areas, where is it going? Here are a couple of places.
- NAMB leased a fire truck and paid an outside media firm to drive it through towns to advertise the Elevate conferences. Elevate lost more than $600,000 of mission-designated money the first year,[69] but NAMB scheduled two more conferences the following year, for

---

[68] http://misfityouthworker.blogspot.com/2006/o4/well-i-asked-for-feedback-on-namb.html.
[69] Taken from strategic reserves.

another $400,000 loss. I'm not sure what leasing an old fire truck costs. Maybe not a lot. But what would it take to allow an Idaho church staff member to concentrate on the Lord's work at night instead of cleaning toilets?
- NAMB mission dollars paid for generous severance packages for Chuck Allen and Bob Reccord. Bob Reccord took an attorney into his "transition negotiations" and made sure he left NAMB financially heeled with the sacrificial gifts of contributors nationwide. Sources said Bob got $.5 million, two years' health benefits, and $12,000 to pay an employment agency to find him a new job.

When trustees were questioned about the half million dollar severance, chairman Bill Curtis dodged a direct answer but replied that "there is precedent at other SBC agencies" for such a severance package. The *Associated Baptist Press* reported that there was "no uniform practice for awarding severance to SBC agency executives who leave under pressure—and most settlements are not reported in detail."[70] They went on to give examples of four Southern Baptist leaders who were pressured into taking early retirement or were dismissed. One was given a year's salary, one 18 months' salary, one a $40,000 severance package, and one "full salary for an undisclosed period of time, then approximately half of his annual pay in retirement, in addition to health insurance and other benefits."[71]

Clearly, Southern Baptists pay generously to remove leaders who, in someone's opinion, aren't doing their jobs. When Chuck and Bob were discovered to be misspending God's money, NAMB paid hundreds of thousands of dollars to get them to leave. As one retiree put it, "If you do a good job, work hard, and finish the

---

[70] "NAMB 'moving on' after resignation, but won't disclose Reccord's severance," by Greg Warner, ABPnews.com, May 2, 2006.
[71] Ibid.

course, you get a plaque. If you use NAMB money fraudulently, you get a generous severance."
- After Bob's resignation, "NAMB terminated a relationship with 316 Networks, a broadband Internet site that already cost the agency $1.4 million but had only generated $30,000. Trustees said it would have cost an additional $2 million and there was little hope it would ever be profitable."[72]

  The 316 Network was highly publicized by Bob at the 2005 annual SBC meeting. Money was poured into this three-way business deal among NAMB, InovaOne, and an Atlanta hosting business. But apparently, no one checked out the competition, and 316 Networks soon found itself competing with another site, hosted by the same company, www.streamingfaith.com, which was already established among churches.
- After Bob left NAMB, auditors discovered that payments were being made to evangelist Jay Strack ($300,000) and Bob's mega-pastor Johnny Hunt at Woodstock Baptist Church ($92,000). Final payments were sent after Bob resigned but before he left the building. Hunt's checks were for the "Timothy-Barnabas Schools," but there were no written contracts.

  So nearly half a million dollars was paid to Strack and Hunt through verbal agreements with Bob. These men were two of the 41 leaders who signed the public letter affirming Bob.
- Another of the 41, Hayes Wicker, First Baptist Church, Naples, Florida, invited Bob to speak at his church about a month before Bob stepped down as NAMB president. According to a church member, immediately after Bob spoke, Wicker "strongly promoted" Bob's most recent book and encouraged every Sunday School class to (per the church member) "stop what they were studying, buy

---

[72] "NAMB trustees begin charting new course for agency," by Joe Westbury, *The Christian Index*, May 4, 2006.

the book and study it, even if they were studying the Bible instead at the time."

Some, I understand, declined, calling the book "boring." But the person sharing the story with me observed, "I found it odd that a pastor would promote the book of his friend that strongly to his congregation."

The camaraderie of the 41 seems laced with quid pro quo.

- NAMB mission money paid $3.3 million in contracts to Bob Reccord's friend, Steve Sanford. And after Bob resigned, Sanford reportedly negotiated a dissolution of just one of the three contracts for a settlement of $1 million.
- While New York missionaries struggled to finance their ministries, Bob supposedly hosted a "think tank" for mega pastors at the Waldorf-Astoria.
- It's impossible to estimate how many mission dollars went directly to the Dumpster. Products printed so hastily that they contained editing errors were simply tossed. And marketing regularly donated huge quantities of unwanted products to overseas missions, paying shipping costs to these ministries.
- Before he received a Blackberry cell phone, Bob had a plethora of cell phones. According to one tech employee, each time Bob's phone dropped a call, even in an out-of-the-way location, he required a new one. An Internet technology staff member estimated contributors paid for a new phone as often as every two months.
- Though Bob stated that Cheryl's personal ministry, Total Life Impact, was totally separate from NAMB, he apparently forgot that NAMB had supplied not only Bob with office, laptop, and home computers, but also a home computer and printer for Cheryl. While many missionaries struggle with antiquated computers and printers, according to NAMB's tech staff, contributors' dollars paid for Bob and Cheryl to have a total of four computer systems, plus a Blackberry.

- In December 2005, mission dollars paid for hardwood floors in NAMB's executive suite and for an office door with Bob's name etched into the glass. Mission dollars would be used to replace the door when Bob stepped down just months later.
- In December 2005, as staff were being terminated, mission dollars were spent for evangelism staff and state evangelism directors—and their spouses—to take a cruise to the Bahamas. (One staff member was reportedly informed of her pending termination while on the cruise.) On at least two occasions, HMB staff attempted to take cruises to Alaska and the Bahamas but, as a former HMB staff member said, "It was nipped in the bud."

    NAMB evangelism staff had already begun planning a second cruise before information about extravagance surfaced.
- Over just a few months, 147,000 sacrificial dollars were spent for private jets. Rumor spread that on at least one occasion, Bob was offered a free Angel Flight to view the Hurricane Katrina damage. Rumor spread that he chose a private jet instead.

    When Bob left, NAMB found itself 18 months into a four-year contract with InovaOne Aviation. Trustees quickly terminated the relationship, saving $40,000 in unused pilot hours and aircraft maintenance. However, they still had to pay for air hours they would not be using.
- Cooperative Program dollars were spent for basketball courts, batting cages, and rock climbing walls to lure people into the NAMB exhibit at the annual Southern Baptist Convention meetings. Though the exhibit was always crowded, it was often filled with preteen boys entertaining themselves while their parents visited other exhibits.

    During the early NAMB years, we spent more and more on theatrics with no measurable results. One year, missionaries rappelled from the auditorium rafters during the NAMB annual report time.

People will always try to push the envelope, and some will get anything they can. One HMB staff member attempted to be reimbursed for condoms, *but the reimbursement was denied.* The difference is leaders. Strong ones will stop irresponsible spending. Weak or absent ones lower the standards and open the doors for others to follow.

Cost to negotiate a close to just one of InovaOne's three contracts after Bob Reccord's resignation: $1 million

What could Idaho Baptists do with a million dollars?

Section 4   The Ghost of Giving Future

Chapter 12
Staying the Course

Let's dream a little about super-sized churches and agencies. What will happen if they continue as they are now?

Are their days numbered?

After a particularly frustrating day at NAMB, I once vented to a retired staff member who stopped by to say hi.

"If NAMB continues like it's going, it will fold before I retire."

My friend replied, "Mary, you're overly optimistic. NAMB won't be around that long."

At the time, I thought my friend was exaggerating to make a point. But that was before the trustee audit and Bob Reccord's resignation. After those events, the thought of NAMB closing its doors seemed feasible.

In 1997, some Southern Baptist agencies were found to be unnecessary and were either dissolved or merged with others. So why should NAMB be guaranteed an existence? The question is, How important are NAMB and other mega religious agencies to accomplishing the Great Commission? With NAMB fully funding only 32 missionary families on a $126 million budget and individual churches excited and effective in sharing Christ from Jerusalem to the uttermost parts of the earth, may I suggest that they are not crucial.

After Bob Reccord prolonged his resignation and dragged NAMB through unnecessary bad press, he made this comment to an associate when he heard I was writing a book: "I just hope the book doesn't hurt NAMB and its ministries." This was my initial concern as well. However, as I've studied not only NAMB's weaknesses but also the amazing strengths of churches, small ministries, and even some mega ministries, I have come to the conclusion that agencies like NAMB are not necessarily synonymous with missions, and super-sized doesn't guarantee super effectiveness.

Someone assured Bob that I wouldn't write anything unkind because I loved NAMB and I loved the missionaries. I don't love NAMB and its work. I love God and His work, which includes His servants. If NAMB is doing God's work, telling the truth won't stop it. If they're following their own egos, nothing can save them.

For too long, Christians have tried to hide their sin from the rest of the world, some even using the excuse that we're protecting God's name.

I believe God wants us to confront sin, just as Joshua confronted Achan when he stole from the spoils of Jericho.[73] I believe it's up to everyday Christians to pull up the rocks and shine a spotlight under them. We need to say to the world, "Money is sometimes misused and some leaders are behaving in ungodly ways. But we are not all like that, and we have the courage to deal with those who are."

It's my conclusion that God doesn't need NAMB and neither do Southern Baptists. To fulfill the Great Commission, why not take a hard look at the most efficient way to do it?

Cutting out the middle man

I teach a Sunday School class of more than 50 men and women in their 50s and 60s. I could write volumes about the hands-on missions and ministries carried out regularly by these incredible saints. Not long ago, some couples from our class

---

[73] Joshua 7. In the midst of an "embarrassing" military defeat, Joshua feigned (v. 9) concern for God's great name. God commanded him to confront Israel's sin.

purchased their own plane tickets for a mission trip to Tanzania, where they assisted Ministry Through Education in building classrooms for a Christian school.

Our class sent them on their trip with cash to purchase 100 bicycles for local pastors. Each volunteer took one suitcase of clothes to wear (which most left for the locals) and one suitcase of new or nearly new clothing to distribute.

When our class members returned, we used a Sunday School hour to allow them to share their mission experiences so all of us could learn firsthand about African missions and see how our financial contributions were used.

One of the men, Larry, told us: "I took some old gardening shoes with me to wear when we were doing construction work. By the time we were ready to go home, the soles were falling off the shoes, so I tossed them in the trash. One of the locals asked me to take them out of the trash because someone would need them.

"A few minutes later, a local pastor entered the room, saw the shoes, and rushed to pick them up. He asked if they were taken. When he learned they were available, he said, 'I've been praying that God would give me shoes, and He's answered my prayers.'"

I couldn't forget that story. The woman who coordinated Ministry Through Education and the trip to Tanzania was my good friend Margaret Burks. Margaret's 91st birthday was coming up in August, and I asked God to allow me to give her 91 pairs of shoes to pack into suitcases the next time she took a group to Tanzania.

A few months later, my mom and I were driving back from lunch near her home in Kentucky when we saw a "store closing" sign.

"Want to check it out?" I asked. With an energy level equal to someone 30 years younger than her 83 years, I knew Mom's answer would be "sure."

We found ourselves in the middle of an auction. The auctioneer was getting ready to auction a stack of wire bins filled with shoes.

"I need those shoes!" I nearly shouted to Mom. "I need them for my friend to take to Africa."

A lady overheard me. "You have to register outside and get a number to bid."

I was frantic. "I don't have time! They're the next item up for auction. I need those shoes!"

The lady offered to let me bid and use her number to pay for the shoes if I won.

After a brief frenzy of bidding, I won the shoes for $13. Mom and I took them back to her apartment and counted them. One hundred forty-six pairs of sturdy leather and rubber sandals with Velcro straps to adjust length and width, ranging in sizes from infant to a man's size 12. Mixed with the shoes were more than a dozen boys' shirts. It was far more than I'd asked of God.

Mom and I habitually have fun when I visit, but finding the shoes will always be a highlight for us. The shoes cost less than 9 cents a pair. Since our car was full, Mom stored them in her small apartment closet until our daughter, Penny, visited a few months later. Penny filled her trunk with bags of shoes and delivered them to Georgia free of charge. Volunteers packed them in their suitcases when they paid their own ways to Africa. Thirteen dollars. Absolutely no overhead.

Imagine the costs that would have been involved to have the International Mission Board get 146 pairs of shoes to Africa. Imagine the cost to have the North American Mission Board get 146 pairs of shoes to Appalachia. Personnel time, storage, travel expenses or shipping, and probably at least $10 per pair to purchase the shoes. And don't forget the cost of sending reporters and camera crews to document the deed. We'd be talking thousands of dollars. And writing a check could never equal the excitement and fulfillment of buying those shoes.

It's experiences like this that make me think that large agencies need us more than we need them. And when more of us figure that out, we'll redirect our money to more fulfilling and effective uses.

Whitewashing

Each time we hear a Jim Bakker, Jimmy Swaggart, or Bob Reccord story we realize how little our sacrificial gifts mean to them and how far a small ministry can stretch our dollars.

As contributors are treated more and more like children, with sugarcoated press releases, secret severance packages, and "out of the box leader" used to describe insubordination and self-indulgence, fewer and fewer of us want to trust big agencies with our sacrificial dollars.

When NAMB trustees whitewashed Bob's indiscretions,[74] they sent some powerful messages:

(1) We'll do whatever it takes to keep our Sunday best showing to the public.

(2) We're more concerned with secular criticism than getting God's work done. Jesus apparently had no concerns that the secular press would pick up on the trouble in the temple when He turned over the tables of the money changers. He saw misuse in God's house and He dealt with it.

While I'm not even the third cousin of a prophet, the future's not hard to imagine. When I dream of the future of Christian evangelism and ministry—if we continue as we are now, here's what I see.

The future

As we focus on a few "celebrities" and give them the power they crave, we'll continue to have leaders who spend our contributions on ego-building self-promotion. A. Larry Ross Communications and the DeMoss Group, perhaps the two largest and most prestigious Christian public relations firms, list as their clients many of the agencies and para-church groups

---

[74] NAMB trustees continued to affirm Reccord, stating that his job was not in jeopardy, even after many concerns surfaced. On the positive side, they have since taken giant steps to reduce the possibility of a similar situation developing in the future.

that receive millions in contributor dollars. Some groups are listed on both sites. The Ross website lists one of their services as "reputation management." Aren't we supposed to manage our own reputations by staying out of trouble?[75] As a former marketing director, I realize the value of promoting products and emphases. But branding individuals and managing reputations takes us to another realm.

    The more average Christians become aware that a small group of king bees use their money to accomplish personal dreams, the less likely they'll be to continue handing over their contributions. Smart people will want their money to count for the Kingdom. And since a tiny handful of leaders can't do it without the money of the masses, they'll only stay in operation if we continue to relinquish the financial privileges and responsibilities entrusted to us.

    Some people will continue to give to large agencies because it's simply easier. While these agencies may experience increased financial struggles, they'll hang on till the last minute, just as Bob hung onto NAMB. And there will always be supporters, like the 41 who shamelessly signed the letter absolving Bob of wrongdoing.

    But I believe ego-driven organizations will operate without God. God doesn't change. He expects total commitment not only from the rich young ruler, but also from agencies and para-churches that operate in His name. When I was still at NAMB, I heard more than once from coworkers who felt that soon God would take His hand off NAMB. Others felt He already had.

    Agencies and para-church groups that detach themselves from God's will and rely more and more on their personal agendas will find that "all the good people" will continue to leave. Many dedicated individuals struggle at ailing churches and agencies, praying daily that their organizations will turn around. But eventually, I believe, God will call them to other ministries.

---

[75] www.demossgroup.com and www.alarryross.com.

As some people continue giving to Paul Bunyan-sized agencies and see no results, they'll come to believe that our nation and the world are unreachable. Eventually they'll stop giving altogether.

But God's work won't stop. If agencies-on-steroids continue as they are—run on politics and egos—they may eventually go the way of the passenger pigeon, but God's work will continue until He comes again. And individuals, churches, and even some large agencies and para-churches will find where He's working and join Him.

From the ashes

Bob Reccord wanted to brand himself, and in a sense, he has. His name is now right up there with Bakker and Swaggart, synonymous with extravagance and self-indulgence. Unfortunately, he's taken NAMB down that branding road with him.

But the truth is that NAMB could become the safest mega agency to give to. It's now been publicly exposed and scrutinized. Southern Baptists will be watching it more closely than ever before. Trustees will hold themselves accountable for more than a couple of sugarcoated trips to Georgia.

I once heard the story of an employee who made a mistake that cost his company tens of thousands of dollars. The employee's supervisor asked the president if he should fire him.

"No," said the president. "Promote him."

Then he explained to the stunned supervisor. "He'll never make a mistake like that again."

If NAMB is conscientious, it can rise from Bob's ashes to become an agency that's beyond reproach. But it will have to turn its ship around and have a new plan of action. It can, and I hope it will. But right now, the *Christian Index* article describes it accurately. It's "hanging in the balance." And only time will tell who it chooses to serve.

Chapter 13
Turning the Ship Around

I served the first year of NAMB as a strategist in mission education. One of the features in the younger boys magazine was two pages of readers' drawings. One day, our editor came into my office with one of the drawings.

"How prophetic is this?" she asked. We all knew that RAs, the boys organization, was struggling and should have been revamped or eliminated years ago.

The child's drawing was titled "Get onboard with RAs" and featured a ship. Across the side of the ship was written "*Titanic*." RAs was just one of NAMB's many sinking ships that no one seemed to notice.

Heed warnings

Big ships turn slowly, but they can turn with proper warning. The real *Titanic* sank in the early morning hours of April 13, 1912. On the afternoon of April 12, about 1:45 p.m., the steamer *Amerika*, warned the *Titanic* that large icebergs were in its path. For some reason, the warnings never made it to the bridge (the forward part of the ship where the navigational crew works). That evening, the ship *Mesaba* sent another message. Again it failed to reach the bridge. And still later, around 10:00 p.m., the *Californian* sent a frantic message to the *Titanic*, warning them of icebergs. The radio operators were busy sending messages for the wealthy and famous passengers and they sharply warned the *Californian* not to interrupt.

At 11:40, the *Titanic* crew spotted a large iceberg directly in front of the ship. The crew tried to reverse the engines and turn the ship, but it was too late.

Face problems head on

Some experts say that if the ship had faced its opponent head on, it would not have sunk. Instead, the crew waited too long, and then did a little sidestep. The iceberg simply brushed the starboard side of the ship, but it buckled the hull and popped out rivets below the waterline. The *Titanic* had six watertight compartments, and at least two needed to be intact to keep the ship afloat. Five quickly filled with water. It was inevitable that the ship would sink.

The officers knew the ship would sink, but they wanted to avoid alarming the passengers. Instead of sounding an emergency alarm, they discreetly went from cabin to cabin, knocking on doors and suggesting that people put on their life jackets and come to the main deck. Some passengers thought the entire episode was a joke.

Wake up

When the first lifeboat was launched an hour after the collision, only 28 of the 65 seats were filled. Disbelieving passengers continued to enjoy the evening's festivities. And when the emergency finally struck home, those onboard the sinking ship learned that lifeboats were limited. The original plans for the *Titanic* were to have 32 lifeboats, but the decision-makers decided that two rows of lifeboats spoiled the lines of the ship. They reduced the number to 20.

Two hours and 40 minutes after the collision, the *Titanic* sank, carrying 2,295 of the 3,000 passengers and crew to their death. [76]

When a crew member was asked at the start of the voyage if the *Titanic* was unsinkable, he said, "God Himself could not sink this ship." But misjudgment and overconfidence took it down and took it down savagely.

---

[76] http://www.gma.org/space1/titanic.html and
http://en.wikipedia.org/wiki/RMS_Titanic.

On the outside, the *Titanic* appeared unsinkable. But it was the danger beneath the surface that caused her to sink. One of Bob Reccord's books is entitled *Beneath the Surface*, and the cover illustration is an iceberg. The subtitle of the book is "steering clear of the dangers that could leave you shipwrecked."

The *Titanic* was equipped with state-of-the-arts technology of its day. Its crew was experienced and skilled. Money was no object in building it. So what missteps caused the *Titanic* to sink?

How can an agency sink?

Caring more about appearances than safety contributed to the disaster. It's what caused management to cut the number of lifeboats nearly in half. And it's what caused the crew to quietly instruct passengers to put on lifejackets instead of sounding an alarm. When NAMB trustees chose to express their support of Bob, even after their own 19-page report revealed irresponsible spending, they sent the message that appearance was more important than getting the ship back on course. Any agency that decides to gloss over indiscretions "for appearances sake" could find itself in danger.

The *Titanic* sank because its leaders failed to heed repeated warnings. An organization that ignores warnings has only itself to blame when the warnings finally stop.

The *Titanic* failed to face the problem head on, and so did NAMB. So do many other agencies.

Titanic passengers failed to take the warnings seriously. They allowed lifeboats to leave with vacant seats because they found it impossible to believe that a ship as great at the *Titanic* could sink. You and I are passengers onboard many great denominational agency and para-church voyages, and it's up to us to heed the warnings. Powerful ships can sink.

Vision

Lack of visibility and lack of time are hindrances to turning any ship around. If we can't or won't look forward, we won't see an obstacle. And if we wait too late, big ships turn slowly.

The dangers to responsible giving are directly in our path. With vision, we can see them. And if we care more about serving God than appearances, we can address the issues head on.

Closeness

It's true that Moses and Aaron led the children of Israel in a responsible collection of gold and silver for the tabernacle, but the same people followed Aaron in collecting jewelry for a golden calf. The same mega group got it right one time and wrong the next. One difference was in the leader. And it's harder to know and monitor the leader of an agency or para-church that's far from you.

It's true that a leader can operate without integrity in a small agency as easily as in a large one. But leaders close to you are easier to scrutinize.

And it's true that Jesus gave responsible stewards increased responsibility (Matt. 25:23). There's nothing dishonorable about being the leader of a mega-church, large agency, or para-church. It can be a great privilege and an opportunity to serve God in a large way.

Too big to scrutinize

But the structure of organizations like NAMB make it nearly impossible to ensure consistent and long-term checks and balances. Leaders come and go, and they operate with varied degrees of self-indulgence. Trustees sweep through four to 12 times a year, so it's easy to put up facades and difficult for trustees to know the hard questions to ask.

In an XXL agency it's hard to know consistently what's going on in every part of the organization. Those who are aware of inappropriate operations are often afraid to speak up, or they speak up and no one listens. In the 22 years I served on the staff of a large church and in two national agencies, I saw the best and the worst. I saw money used carefully and money wasted. But the money continued to come in, regardless of who was in charge and how they were using the money.

Turning the ship around means setting tough scrutiny guidelines for large agencies. Many have realized this need in the past. Campus Crusade for Christ International and the Billy Graham Evangelistic Association are charter members of the Evangelistic Council for Financial Accountability.[77] Agencies that do it right don't mind being scrutinized.

Reversing course

To turn the Southern Baptist ship around, 16 million of us have to stop supplying the resources for 35 people to live their dreams and feed their egos. Some of these 35 lead their churches to give less than average. Each year, as the SBC elects its president, the issue of Cooperative Program giving within the candidates' churches seems to take a back seat to other issues.[78] Some presidents' churches have been strong givers, and some churches' giving has been abysmal.

While Southern Baptists are the first to tout a democratic leadership, that democracy is most evident in the local church. When the individuals and churches that support the North American Mission Board heard about Bob's resignation, most waited helplessly to see who would be the next president. Those closer to the situation first watched to see who would be elected chairman of trustees. Two candidates were considered. If one were elected, the assumption was that NAMB would have another mega-pastor as its second president. If Bill Curtis were elected (and he was), they'd be more likely to have someone with more balance and denominational experience as president.

---

[77] www.ecfa.org.
[78] With the exception of the 2006 election of Frank Page.

Is there a way for 16 million Southern Baptists to be involved in selecting agency heads? Probably not. The system's just too big. Can 16 million Southern Baptists be involved in selecting their pastors and local mission leaders? You betcha.

To turn the entire ship around, every denomination would have to set up elaborate scrutiny guidelines. They would have to scrutinize thoroughly and often to accommodate constant leader turnover. And how much of God's money would that cost?

I pray that everyone mentioned in these pages will be light years above these difficulties by the time you read this. I believe in redemption and God's ability to change all of us. I believe, as did Ronald Reagan, that "Man is good, that what is right will always triumph, and there is purpose and worth to each and every life."[79] God has the power to strengthen and restore any broken or sinking vessel. All He asks is that we be willing to turn.

But what about the next batch of leaders? Turning the ship around may mean disembarking and taking lots of smaller ships to our destination: fulfillment of the Great Commission.

God ordained the church. I see nothing in the Bible that holds us to a system of mega agencies.

---

[79] Inscribed on former President Ronald Reagan's tomb.

Chapter 14
Call to Change

Do you want to be sure your sacrificial gifts are used wisely? Then it's time to take responsibility for how your money is spent.

Suppose you start today keeping close tabs on how your tithes and offerings are spent? Will it make an eternal difference? Even if you're wealthy and your contributions are large, they can't measure up against the billions of dollars others may continue pouring into deep pockets of misuse. But your actions will matter.

Your small part

Imagine that a stranger approached you one day when you were vacationing at the seashore. He hired you to move sand. He gave you a teaspoon and instructed you to move the sand—one teaspoon at a time—from the beach. You were not to use a bucket or a wheelbarrow. You had to carry each teaspoon of sand across the beach, along the boardwalk, through a big parking lot, and to a dump truck parked in the far corner of the lot. You then had to climb up the side of the dump truck and toss the sand into the bed of the truck.

All the while you were carrying teaspoons of sand, giant waves replenished what you'd carried away. Many times during the day, you wanted to toss the teaspoon into the ocean and give up.

But suppose, at the end of the day, the person who hired you walked right past the tons of sand left on the beach. He climbed into the bed of the truck and carefully swept every grain of the sand you carried and scooped it into a small pile. He looked at the sand and smiled approvingly, saying, "We'll weigh the sand you carried, and I'll give you an equal weight in diamonds."

Suddenly, your focus would switch from the sand left on the beach to the sand in the truck. And the sand you gathered would look glorious.

That's a healthy way to think about following God's instructions. We should look at what we're able to do instead of what doesn't get done.

Call to action

And every once in a while, what we do is like wildfire. Have you ever been around a fire that spread fast? You toss a lit match, and it falls on gasoline. Instead of smoldering a little, it ignites a huge fire that spreads quickly.

That's what happened when Mordecai Ham preached the revival service where Billy Graham was saved. We never know when we'll do something that will inspire others and create a chain reaction. We can't guarantee a wildfire, but we can promise a spark.

Don't you imagine that the person who tells a neighbor about the Lord, even if that neighbor is unresponsive, pleases God as much as Mordecai Ham? God doesn't tell us to do enormous, mind-boggling things. He just tells us to obey and leave the enormous, mind-boggling results to Him.

That's why I had to write this book. God put me in positions where I saw gross misuse of His money. I felt that still small voice instructing me to speak up. The louder voice of reason countered, "No one will listen. And if they listen, they won't care. And if they care, they won't take action."

And eventually I acknowledged that the louder voice was probably correct. But the instructions remained: "Speak up. Carry your part of the sand. And maybe others on the beach will join you."

I challenge you to join me in scrutinizing those who spend God's money. Many operate responsibly. Some don't. It's our responsibility to choose the recipients of our contributions as carefully as we would choose any other business partner.

I challenge you to know how your money is being spent. At the very least, demand an accounting of the dollars you've sacrificed to give. Organizations that operate with integrity aren't afraid to show you a detailed line-by-line budget.

I challenge you to give more than ever before, only wisely. Never have the needs been so great. Never have our contributions been so necessary. Don't you dare take the information in this book as an excuse to stop giving. Don't read something that's not on these pages. Don't hear something I'm not saying.

I challenge you to join me in responsible giving, even if you and I stand alone.

Evangelist Henry Varley once said to D.L. Moody: "The world is yet to see what God can do with, for, through and in a man who is fully consecrated to Him."

Moody answered: "By the Holy Spirit in me, I'll be that man."[80]

---

[80] www.wholesomewords.org, Christian Biography Resources, "Why God Used D.L. Moody," by R.A. Torrey.

Chapter 15
Newsworthy

Operating with integrity is an unnatural process. It's only when Christ fills our lives in a supernatural way that we serve with an unselfish spirit. Even then, it's a continual struggle and as Bob inscribed in my copy of his book, we must guard our hearts.

Pastors and leaders who live what they preach make a conscious effort to guard against self-indulgence and a mind-set of entitlement. These weaknesses can surface in a soup kitchen or a $126 million denominational agency. And though inappropriate behavior on a large scale in a plus-size agency wastes more of God's money, all misuse is wrong.

We often hear about those who misuse God's money because the media is looking for unusual stories. And with so much attention on wasteful spending, it's easy to become discouraged. Yet all over the world—from New York to Hawaii, from Tokyo to Tanzania—you'll find people putting service to God above material wealth.

It's not difficult to find positive examples to follow and honest agencies to receive our contributions. Here are some not-so-unusual agencies and churches that are, to me, newsworthy.

24 percent to missions

Pastor Shawn Murphy leads Calvary Chapel International Worship Center in Severn, Maryland. Their average Sunday morning attendance is 200. They have more than 50 ministries, including a local food distribution ministry and international ministries to Africa and India.

Pastor Shawn realizes that a Christian leader's salary requires a balance between providing adequately (Luke 10:7) and elevating to an inappropriate level.

"It's important to respect Christian leaders," says Pastor Shawn. "Jesus was unable to do mighty works in His hometown because He wasn't respected.

"But sometimes respect moves to material respect. Some people want to live vicariously through someone they look up to. They want pastors and leaders to have nice things. Soon we're operating on worldly standards with pastors having the best cars and the nicest houses. But the shepherd's there for the sheep."

Pastor Shawn evaluates himself on Ezekiel 34:1-10 (New Living Translation): "Then this message came to me from the LORD: 'Son of man, prophesy against the shepherds, the leaders of Israel. Give them this message from the Sovereign LORD: Destruction is certain for you shepherds who feed yourselves instead of your flocks. Shouldn't shepherds feed their sheep?

"'You drink the milk, wear the wool, and butcher the best animals, but you let your flocks starve.

"'You have not taken care of the weak. You have not tended the sick or bound up the broken bones. You have not gone looking for those who have wandered away and are lost. Instead, you have ruled them with force and cruelty.

"'So my sheep have been scattered without a shepherd. They are easy prey for any wild animal.

"'They have wandered through the mountains and hills, across the face of the earth, yet no one has gone to search for them.

"'Therefore, you shepherds, hear the word of the LORD: As surely as I live, says the Sovereign LORD, you abandoned my flock and left them to be attacked by every wild animal. Though you were my shepherds, you didn't search for my sheep when they were lost. You took care of yourselves and left the sheep to starve.

"'Therefore, you shepherds, hear the word of the LORD. This is what the Sovereign LORD says: I now consider these shepherds my enemies, and I will hold them responsible for what has happened to my flock. I will take away their right to feed the flock, along with their right to feed themselves. I will rescue my flock from their mouths; the sheep will no longer be their prey.'"

"I start with the heart before the head," explains Pastor Shawn. "And Ezekiel 34 is the best Scripture I know to keep my heart in check. It's God's message to His leaders. It's easy to accept the world's standards of success. But it's not about me. If the devil can trick me into thinking it's about me, everything else fails.

"I have a responsibility to the sheep. Ezekiel 34 keeps my heart on track and my accountant keeps my head on track." All ministers at Calvary are evaluated periodically for, among other things, how they use the church's finances.

"Most pastors start out with a pure heart," says Pastor Shawn, "but we can get so involved in the business of the church that we forget that first of all, we're ministers. But we're ministers who need to use strong business principles."

Pastor Shawn is a firm believer in excellence and anointing. "We use an accounting firm that specializes in church finances, one where no church members work. Everything goes through these outside accountants, as well as a stewardship council. The accountants provide a monthly report of every penny that's given or spent.

"We want everyone to understand how church finances are handled, so we share our financial structure in our new member classes."

"It's wise to guard against financial misuse by everyone, including the pastor. It can't be about the pastor's whims. It has to be about God's kingdom," observes Pastor Shawn. "Our church is protected against abuse by the pastor, against the pastor wanting to do his own thing. I have no physical access to finances. I don't count the money, and I don't know the combination to the church safe."

While Pastor Shawn's church has no reason to doubt his honesty, he stresses, "Pastors shouldn't open themselves up to accusations because they don't have everything set up in excellence. We live in a day when you cannot afford to act in ignorance."

Calvary distributes financial responsibility. They have a four-person Presbytery board that sets the pastor's salary and provides counsel on all major financial decisions. The Presbytery has the right to put the pastor under its authority for counseling or removal, if appropriate.

Working under the pastor is a stewardship council made up of elders and church members with business experience. "There's safety in a multitude of counselors," admonishes Pastor Shawn.

Besides ensuring wise financial stewardship, Calvary also encourages all its members to become involved in hands-on ministries. They've adopted Rick Warren's[81] slogan of "every member a minister."

"We put ministries before the church in an intentional way," says Pastor Shawn. "We keep members informed, and we develop a vision they can feel a part of. People will give one-time toward a need, but they'll live full-time toward a vision.

"People are stirred to give when they see starving children on television. That's good, and it's needed. But we also need to impart a vision, to instill a kingdom vision and mentality. That's what moves Christians to become disciples.

"Calvary helps impart a vision by bringing our missionaries in at least once a month to share what they're doing and how they're spending our money. Whether it's a new heating system or Bibles, we need to know."

"We encourage everyone to get involved in the vision, even if it's in a small way," says Pastor Shawn. "There's something about spiritual success. It breathes life into the vision, and it helps everyone continue serving and giving. Last year, 24 percent of our budget went to missions."

Calvary members spend mission dollars through hands-on projects, but they also give to outside ministries. Before asking his church to give to a particular ministry, Pastor Shawn investigates the ministry personally.

---

[81] Rick Warren is pastor of Saddleback Community Church and author of *The Purpose-Driven Church* and *The Purpose-Driven Life.*

"After Hurricane Katrina, church members wanted to give to the relief," says Pastor Shawn. "We called each agency to see how much money went to meet the need and how much went to administration. It varied greatly. We eventually found a ministry that used 98 percent of contributions for hurricane victims and only 2 percent for administration. That's the one we went with."

"You have to research," says Pastor Shawn. "The Bible says, 'Know those who labor among you.'[82] Except for one-time gifts to people who speak at our church, we only give to missionaries we're in relationship with. We take seriously that we have to know the ministries our people give to. Most of the ministries we've asked church members to give to, either I or our Presbyters have personally visited."

Is he 100 percent sure their gifts are used wisely? "As long as man is man," answers Pastor Shawn, "there will be financial abuses. If we stop giving to all ministries because man has failed us, we'll be in trouble.

"Man will fail us. We'll always hear of financial abuses, but it shouldn't stop us from giving. Someday, we'll stand before the Lord and give account.

"If we become like the man who hid what he had in the ground, not giving because we don't trust ministries, we'll be unrighteous servants."

Cautious but liberal giving

My husband, Jack, and I were privileged to take a cruise to Hawaii last year. The ship docked at Kona for a day, and we visited Hawaii's oldest Christian church, Mokuaikaua Church.

When we stepped into the small old sanctuary, we were immediately impressed by the way money was and was not used. While the building was well-kept in a way that honored God, it was truly functional. Reminders of why the church existed were everywhere. On one side, along the wall, was a

---

[82] 1 Thessalonians 5:12, New American Standard Bible.

box filled with old baby bottles, with instructions to take one home, fill it with coins, and return the money to be used to purchase baby supplies for the crisis pregnancy center.

In the back of the sanctuary was a poster with photos of the 15 missionary families the church partially supports. Strips of yarn connected the photos to areas on a world map, indicating where each family served.

Mokauikaua Church supports local missions, including feeding homeless people, distributing food and clothing to poor people, helping unwed mothers, and ministering at Big Island Prison. And they support missionaries in the Hawaiian Islands, the Micronesian Islands, France, Spain, Kazakhstan, and the Middle East. All of this is done through direct and personal contact.

Mokuaikaua maintains financial integrity through an annual budget, quarterly financial statements, and daily accounting, with financial responsibilities spread among a treasurer, an accountant, a bookkeeper, an assistant bookkeeper, and a board of trustees. All these people understand the accounting system, and they are all involved in managing and administering the budget. Members can question the budget and give input "any time and anywhere."

Dr. Henry Boshard leads Mokuaikaua congregation and relies on Deuteronomy 16:17, Proverbs 3:9, Luke 18:12, Romans 12:1, and 2 Corinthians 9:7 as guidelines in leading his church to give to God's work. They create their budget on faith. If they feel God leading, they move forward and trust Him to supply their needs.

The church gives generously and joyfully. The 225-member congregation not only gives to international missions; they also provide well for their own church. With 350-500 Sunday worshipers—most of the extras are tourists—repairs and renovations on the old building can be costly. Members gave a half million dollars over the past five years to keep their church building in good shape.

Dr. Boshard's philosophy for spending God's money is this: "We deal cautiously with huge expenditures and liberally when helping the poor and needy."

100 percent to missions

Ministry Through Education, Inc., is a small organization run from Flowery Branch, Georgia. Its secretary/treasurer is 92-year-old CPA Margaret Burks. Last year, Margaret made multiple trips to Tanzania, Malaysia, and Russia. She paid for all her travel expenses, including airline tickets, from her personal checking account. One hundred percent of the money you give to MTE goes to reach people for Christ. The organization uses volunteers to build and repair classrooms for all levels of school—from preschool to seminary, to teach classes at all levels, and to minister to whatever needs they find.

Margaret is amazing. She holds business degrees from Emory University and the University of Georgia. And at 75—a time when most people have been retired for 10 or more years—Margaret answered God's call to enroll in seminary. She's a former International Mission Board missionary who decided time and money could be used more wisely by leading people into direct hands-on ministry.

Though Margaret is a CPA, MTE also retains an outside CPA to conduct yearly audits and file tax returns. But the simplest way MTE makes sure money isn't misspent by staff members (whom they call trustees) is that staff members do not receive salaries and they are not reimbursed for any expenses, including travel.

Volunteers also pay their own ways. As volunteers travel to international mission points and experience firsthand the culture, the needs of the people, and the religious practices, they gain an excitement and understanding unlike anything that can be gained from books, brochures, and videos.

"We firmly believe," says Margaret, "that all we have belongs to God, and we are just His stewards in managing and using His money. So we must use it wisely and in accordance with His will. We have no temptation to use the gifts we receive for anything other than His glory."

With no money going for salaries and staff members' expenses, I feel secure that every penny of my contribution goes to provide Christian education for eager learners like those described in the MTE brochure: "Young African men leave homes that range from barest shelters made of cow dung plastered on a framework of sticks to urban apartments. They share a common goal and a commitment that takes first place in their lives. All have a burning desire to learn how to teach friends and neighbors about Jesus Christ. ... These young Christians come with their Bibles and little more than the clothes they are wearing. Some walk for days in sandals cut from auto tire tread and laced with cord or rawhide."

MTE takes contributions seriously. "The money is spent exactly as requested by the donor," says Margaret, "And if there is no specific request, we spend it on the most urgent need at the time, such as scholarships, student work funds, or for building additional classrooms. To ensure that money is used carefully when it reaches other countries, scholarships are administered through seminaries and universities and not given directly to individual students. We investigate local accountability before providing assistance."

MTE has no budget. They operate solely on a "faith basis." Their records are open for inspection at all times. They open a separate account for every donor, showing the donor's information, the amount given, how the money was designated to be used, and when and how every penny is spent. Those of us who have given to MTE find Margaret's thank-you notes both amusing and reassuring, when they contain a list similar to this:

> *Tuition for Kavira Langat of Kenya $105.00*
> *Building supplies for one primary classroom: $23.72*
> *Remainder of $21.28 will be used toward books for Philip Kaniki of Uganda*

Contributions are always 100 percent accounted for. I've yet to feel led to travel to Africa with Margaret, but I feel that my contributions to MTE put me right there.

Stand and be counted

Over the years, my family and I have moved several times, and finding a church home has always been high priority as we've settled in a new community. While I've known church visitors who asked hard questions about budget and polity, we've found that the heart of a church is usually evident by simply listening and observing. Hearing the Sunday School lesson and the pastor's sermon will quickly tell visitors where the church stands on the moderate/conservative spectrum. Notes in the bulletin will tell how the money is spent, including what percentage is given to local, national, and international missions. And announcements and reminders will tell you how involved members are in hands-on missions and where they place their priorities.

And just meeting the church staff and church members will give you a strong indication of their dedication and sincerity. There's something reassuring about looking church leaders in the eye, asking them questions face-to-face, and getting to know them as friends.

The system is by no means foolproof and the local church is certainly not perfect. Our current church has had four pastors in the 12 years we've worshiped and served there. One came in with an attitude of arrogance and entitlement. But since members worked closely with him, it didn't take long for his attitude to become evident. And he was quickly asked to leave.

When we sought a new pastor, I was serving on the personnel committee. We interviewed prospective pastors identified by the pastor search committee. And when we'd found the one we felt was "God's man for Concord," every person in the church had an opportunity to meet him face to face. He preached a trial sermon. We had a lunch after the worship service, where members asked the hard questions. And every member had the opportunity to vote for or against calling him to our church.

Our current pastor, Dr. Dan Armistead, leads our church in hands-on mission involvement. Youth groups have been to China and senior adults to Africa. Mission groups, Sunday School classes, and individuals sponsor children in a children's home, help with a crisis pregnancy center, minister at the local jail, and work with a transitional home for women with mental illness or drug dependency—just to name a few ways Concord members touch their community and the world with the message of Christ.

Our church is relatively small—a couple hundred in Sunday School each week—but Dan is more interested in starting churches and ministries than creating a mega church.

"All our money shouldn't be spent on ourselves," he observes. "We need good facilities, but we don't need a marble palace. Instead of pouring money into brick and mortar, we want to put money into missions."

In his 20-plus years of ministry, Dan has witnessed people who have given sacrificially to missions.

"I remember a husband who decided to give his wife a new car for Christmas," says Dan. "They weren't wealthy people, and a new car was a big deal. But the couple decided at the last minute to wait another year or two for a new car and give the money to international missions.

"I've seen others who have downsized vehicles and postponed vacations to give to mission projects."
With individuals giving sacrificially, Dan realizes the responsibility of making sure their money is spent wisely. I asked him how he helped ensure financial integrity at Concord. "We run everything by the church," answered Dan. "It's not the easiest road, but it's the healthiest one in the long run."

Dan gives direction to financial situations, but he makes no decisions by himself. Every financial decision goes through at least one—and usually more than one—committee. Major decisions are brought before the church. I consider Dan creative, energetic, and—yes—entrepreneurial. Yet, unlike Bob, he manages to work within a financial system.

"We don't want any hint of immorality or questionable ethics," says Dan. "Jesus told us in Matthew 10:27 [NIV] 'what I tell you in the dark, speak in the daylight; what is whispered in your ear, proclaim from the roofs.' We don't sweep anything under the rug.

"In one of my former churches, a church staff member having financial problems used a church credit card to pay his cell phone bill. He had every intention of paying back the money, but he shouldn't have used a church credit card for personal use.

"When I discovered what he'd done, I informed the budget committee. We decided not to take the matter before the entire church, but I felt that someone besides me needed to know. I didn't want anyone to think I covered up the situation."

Dr. Dan's family gave him a photo that reminds him to lead Concord with integrity. It's the now-famous photo of a lone Chinese student protestor standing small but fearless in front of a large tank in Tiananmen Square. The caption is "Stand and Be Counted."

"What I'm about is bigger than me," explains Dan. "My job is just to stand on the truth. Crosby, Stills and Nash have a song that mentions the boy in the picture. I don't agree with everything about this musical group, but I appreciate the words to this song: 'Stand and be counted, stand on the truth, stand on your honor, stand and be counted.'"

Good things are happening everywhere

Start by checking the Evangelical Council for Financial Accountability[83] and then doing your own homework. You'll find some organizations—many of them large—that have excellent reputations.

And visit local ministries that seem to operate responsibly. You'll find that most are enthusiastic, frugal, and being used by God to do tremendous things. President Reagan

---

[83] www.ecfa.org.

had a plaque on his desk at the White House that's applicable to Christian ministries: "You can be too big for God to use, but you can't be too small."[84]

---

[84] Stated on tour at the Reagan Library, Simi Valley, California.

Chapter 16
A Plan

Ultimately, the best way to be sure your money is well spent is to spend it yourself. That's not always possible, so we have to be willing to trust someone. Otherwise, we're like the servant who hid his one talent in the ground, afraid even to invest it.

Scrutinize

Since we all cannot personally spend every dollar of our contributions, we need a plan for scrutinizing those who spend on our behalf. Here are a few suggestions that have surfaced as I've researched this book.
- If we pay for it, we have a right to know what it cost. Salaries, severance packages, buildings, and anything else paid with contributor dollars should be public record or at least available upon request, with no hoops to jump through to obtain it. If any organization will not tell you how they're spending *your contributions*, why not give to an organization that will?
- If you're not driving the bus, make sure you know who is. And be sure they're not asleep at the wheel. Check out the involvement of trustees, board of directors, or whoever is assigned to oversee the operations of paid staff. Find out how involved they are. Make sure they're asking the hard questions and not just accepting periodic free trips to the agency's main headquarters.

    Trustees should not have to hold the reins too tightly. If they've hired responsible people and they're asking the hard questions, they should step back and let leaders do what they're hired to do. But they should never step out of the picture.

    Watch how trustees respond when a problem arises. Do they make problems public or try to hide them? As one reader wrote in the Mississippi Baptist newspaper in response to the way NAMB trustees seemed to cover the financial misuse story: "The apparent 'spin' the NAMB trustees put on the bad news may have hurt their credibility and ultimately Southern Baptists' financial support through the Annie Armstrong Easter Offering.

"It appears to me that the NAMB didn't get its money's worth of advice from the outside PR consultants. I learned fifty years ago as a public relations officer at a Baptist college that the best way to deal with institutional bad news is to inform the media first, tell the public the whole true story, and accept responsibility for everything you have done wrong.

"Too bad NAMB hasn't learned that lesson."[85]

NAMB trustees could have taken a no-comment or wait-and-see attitude. Instead, they officially affirmed Bob and stated that his job wasn't in jeopardy. In trying to walk the lukewarm middle road, they both accused Bob and affirmed him in the same media reports.

- Invite mega-agency leaders on annual no-frills visits to real mission sites. No reporters and no photo ops. No fine hotels or four-star restaurants. Live like the missionaries, eat what they eat, ride in their cars.

A friend of mine took a college mission trip to Mexico and worked in one of the poorest areas of the country. She told me that, for months after returning to her suburban home, she couldn't enjoy a soft drink because she kept remembering the faces of hungry children. Maybe no-frills mission trips would have this same effect on leader spending.

---

[85] Letter to the editor, "NAMB 'spin' hurts," by Ralph C. Atkinson, Jr., April 27, 2006, *Baptist Record*, Mississippi state Baptist newspaper.

From here to somewhere great

So our first step to making giving more effective is scrutinizing current agencies. But we have to do more. We have to move away from large agencies and bring giving closer to home.

When asked about older, now-ineffective programs, NAMB VP John Yarbrough's standard response was that we should move on to new ventures but keep "feeding the dinosaurs" until they died off. That's actually pretty good advice for moving away from Godzilla-sized agencies. We can't just let big agencies die a sudden violent death. Too many good people work in them.

But we can feed them less and less until they die of natural causes or shrink to a manageable size. I believe there are a few things that large agencies do well—training international missionaries in the languages and cultures where they'll serve, coordinating overseas assignments, coordinating worldwide chaplaincy, coordinating disaster relief efforts, providing certain trainings, and producing certain printed materials. However, once these jobs are accomplished, the majority of actual work is often better accomplished at a state level or lower.

Wouldn't it be great if we gradually stopped feeding the mega agency dinosaurs, possibly moving 1 percent of our giving each year from national to state/association/church level—until we reduced our national and international agencies to a reasonable size? I believe Southern Baptists could give much less than the current $190 million to national and international cooperative efforts and see no measurable difference in advancing the Kingdom. And if that money were redirected to effective ministries, we could see a positive difference.

Spread the power

The more work done reasonably and effectively on a lower level, the less chance for corruption. Resisting corruption is an incredible battle for those in power. British novelist and playwright Henry Fielding (1707-1754) said,

"Nearly all men can stand adversity, but if you want to test a man's character, give him power."

Power corrupts—it's a cliché because it fits the occasion so often that it's used over and over. So if power corrupts, disseminate the power.

Since it's hard to scrutinize big agencies, keep them small. Even with regular audits, expenditures can be hidden, coded incorrectly, or pulled from other budgets. NAMB always passed its Ernest & Young audit—even with a $1 million slush fund, but all that proved was that the books balanced and everything was accounted for somewhere on paper. Audits do not address the ethical/moral use of funds, only if all funds are accounted for.

At the June 2006 Southern Baptist Convention, a messenger asked the SBC Executive Committee to analyze the spending of all Southern Baptist agencies and institutions receiving support from the Cooperative Program. He asked that the study evaluate administrative budgets—especially reimbursable expense accounts, travel expenses, housing expenses, and "the amount of Cooperative Program dollars, spent, if any, to maintain private residences and staff of those entity executives."[86]

That study was completed and approved by the Southern Baptist Convention Executive Committee in September 2006, to be presented at the 2007 annual meeting. The resulting amendments to SBC documents urged SBC leaders toward greater financial responsibility.[87] While this was a positive start, the documents do not ensure financial integrity. No document, audit, or report can.

---

[86] "SBC Exec. Committee approves fiscal-responsibility amendment," by Hannah Elliott, Sept. 21, 2006, Associated Baptist Press online, www.abpnews.com
[87] ibid.

Roll up your sleeves

If big agencies don't do the work and spend the money competently—here's the hard part—you and I may have to.

Be willing to get involved. When the people rebuilt the wall, nearly everyone pitched in. Nehemiah 4:6 (NKJV) says, "For the people had a mind to work." And with each person doing his or her part, the wall was built and the city was fortified. We've tried accomplishing the Great Commission through super-size agencies, and we've failed. Could we do worse with hands-on involvement?

Sewage treatment

While writing this book, I believe I heard nearly every counter argument possible.

"These are broad strokes. Not every mega agency leader is extravagant and wasteful."

True. But let me offer an example of how poisonous the Bobs of the Christian world can be.

Imagine that someone goes to the refrigerator and pulls out a big glass pitcher of milk. It's so cold that the outside of the pitcher is covered with condensation. You hold out your sparkling glass, eager to enjoy the milk.

But your host leaves the room and comes back with a teaspoon filled with liquid. He pours the liquid into the fresh milk and stirs. It still looks and smells great.

"What was that?" you ask.

"Sewage," replies your host. "But it was just a teaspoon." He pours a glass of milk, hands it to you, and says, "Enjoy!" Though the drink is 99.9 percent milk, what are you drinking?

I've also heard the argument: "Some talented folks work in even the most corrupt mega agency." Very true. Many dedicated Christians watched helplessly as NAMB money was wasted. But there was little they could do.

Imagine that you're seated at another table, and you ask your host for a glass of milk. He leaves the room and returns with a pitcher of dirty foul-smelling liquid.

"What's that?" you ask. He replies, "Sewage."

You gag as he places the pitcher on the table beside you, then takes a carton of milk from the refrigerator and pours a generous cup of the milk into the nasty liquid and stirs. He pours a glass and hands it to you. Your glass of milk was added to the pitcher, but what are you drinking?

It is extremely difficult—though not impossible—to scrutinize large agencies. Waste—even out-and-out dishonesty—can happen in a smaller organization, but it's more easily discovered. Drop a scorpion into a cup and you'll find it quickly. Drop it into a canyon and good luck locating it.

"Big agencies serve a purpose" is another comment I've heard. I believe that statement could be more accurate if it were rephrased: "National agencies serve a purpose, but they don't have to be super big." Some work is better coordinated on a national level, and if we weed out all the work that's duplicated on a lower level or done more effectively by churches and states, the remaining organizations would be national but not necessarily large.

Statistics vary. Exceptions abound. But the basic formula holds true more often than not: The extent of misuse is directly proportionate to the distance between the giver and the spender. And it's up to you and me to reduce the distance.

Appendices

Appendix 1

Emails Received When Leaving NAMB

-----Original Message-----
From: Reccord, Bob <breccord@namb.net>
To: Branson, Mary <mbranson@namb.net>
Sent: Mon May 03 11:02:48 2004
Subject:

Mary
I have been informed of your decision to launch in a new direction and take up the passion to write. I can sure understand your heart, with the passion I have to do the same. I know you will find it challenging, stretching, deepening...and I trust, fulfilling.

Your service here has been greatly appreciated. I think the world of you and Jack and desire the best for both of you in the years ahead. If I can ever help you in any way I would be delighted to do what I can. I believe God has some special things in store for you in the days ahead.

Thanks for all you have done. I thank the Lord for you and your impact. God's grace to you as you go.

-----Original Message-----
From: Allen, Chuck
Sent: Monday, April 26, 2004 8:31 AM

To: Branson, Mary
Subject: RE: PPAM recommendation

Mary,

Thanks for this information. I agree completely with your assessment on the discount.

On another note...I am concerned about your resignation...greatly...you are a gifted and competent leader and I want to be certain that this is your answer to God's will for your life. Should you like, please call me today and let me hear from you.

Be sure that you are sure...you will be missed should you choose to move ahead with your resignation.

Chuck Allen
Chief Operating Officer
North American Mission Board, SBC

-----Original Message-----

From: Adams, Nate
Sent: Tuesday, April 27, 2004 10:39 AM
To: Branson, Mary
Subject: Best wishes
Sensitivity: Confidential

Mary,

I heard about your decision to leave NAMB and wanted you to know that I wish you the best and appreciate all you've contributed to NAMB. Someone told me that you're "retiring" to write and minister in new ways, and that makes me envious!

I left you a voice mail about HR saying that we can do a formal "exit interview" or not, depending on what you and I want to do. (I reminded them that I'm not your current supervisor, but they said they felt I was the best person to do the exit interview given the recency of your transfer to the new Group.) I'd welcome that opportunity if you're open -- it wouldn't have to take a long time. I leave for Nashville tomorrow morning, so it would probably have to be next week. Would you like to schedule something?

- Nate

Appendix 2 Bob Reccord's Resignation and Trustee Chairman Barry Holcomb's Response

NAMB president Bob Reccord resigns; cites 'philosophical and methodological differences' as reasons for parting ways

By Martin King
Apr 17, 2006

ALPHARETTA, Ga. (BP)-- Robert E. Reccord, president of the North American Mission Board, announced his resignation April 17 from the Southern Baptist entity he has led since its creation nine years ago.

Bob Reccord

Speaking to nearly 200 NAMB staff members at NAMB's Atlanta-area offices, Reccord said he made the decision, which was effective immediately, with "mixed emotions."

"I am thankful for the countless numbers of people we have seen come to Christ and the thousands of churches we have seen planted and nurtured," he said. "On the other hand, I regret we were not able to complete a number of things we have started or dreamed about. I regret that events of recent weeks have created an environment which makes it difficult to lead the organization and to stay on mission."

The events Reccord referred to resulted from a lengthy

article two months ago in The Christian Index, newsjournal of the Georgia Baptist Convention. The article, which was critical of the entity's accomplishments and Reccord's leadership, led to an investigation by NAMB's board of trustees which also was critical of some of NAMB's more innovative initiatives and decisions under Reccord's leadership.

During his announcement, Reccord told employees he has found it increasingly difficult to be an entrepreneurial leader within a denominational structure.

"I believe that honest philosophical and methodological differences have brought us to this point of separate directions," Reccord said.

He added he hopes he has "demonstrated my love for and commitment to Southern Baptists and all for which we stand."

"I also hope I have demonstrated a Kingdom heart and mindset," Reccord continued. "It is this mindset and my entrepreneurial bent that have led us to explore more effective applications of technology and media; strategies for reaching a wider range of demographic groups; and creative evangelism initiatives."

Barry Holcomb, chairman of NAMB's board of trustees, read a statement to the mission board's employees, acknowledging Reccord's accomplishments, integrity and visionary leadership style.

"I stand here today with Dr. Reccord to say thank you for nine years of tireless service to the North American Mission Board," Holcomb said. "As an agency, we've seen growth in many areas, including increases in our church planting efforts, a significant increase in mission personnel and the dramatic increase and impact of our disaster relief work."

Holcomb said Reccord had "sought to provide leadership that was both consistent and visionary," and he emphasized that neither a special focused financial audit nor an investigation by the trustees themselves revealed "evidence that Dr. Reccord had done anything unethical in his role as president."

"I believe that important fact has been lost in all the conversation and articles written about the report. Dr. Reccord's integrity is strong and solid today, and I want to emphasize it clearly."

Holcomb said, "Contrary to some opinions, Dr. Reccord is in no way being asked to resign, let alone forced to resign. He is taking this step for what he feels is best for Christ's Kingdom.... I believe that this is one of the strongest evidences of his personal character and integrity."

Holcomb, who is pastor of Bethany Baptist Church in Andalusia, Ala., acknowledged "there are times in the life of every agency when changes are made, not on the basis of crises, but in large part on the basis of vision."

"Dr. Reccord has aptly noted that in [Southern Baptist] Convention life, entrepreneurial leadership and denominational requirements may be at odds with one another. This is no one's fault -- it is simply a reality. There is no question God has some special things in store for the next chapter of this 'out of the box' thinker," Holcomb said.

Reccord told employees he doesn't know what he is going to do but has already received several calls asking him to consider various ministry opportunities.

"We will follow God's leadership to do what is best for the Kingdom," he said.

"Stepping away will allow me to leave behind a never-ending stream of administrative responsibilities and focus on unleashing men, women and young people to fulfill their God-given calling and change the world."

To that end, Holcomb announced that Reccord will serve as a liaison between NAMB and Promise Keepers as he speaks at 19 PK events across the country from June through October.

"NAMB and Promise Keepers entered into an agreement earlier this year to work together to mobilize workers for the rebuild that continues along the Gulf Coast following last year's hurricanes," Holcomb said. "I'm thankful that Dr. Reccord has the opportunity and the desire to challenge Christian men across America to invest their time and talents alongside Southern Baptists."

Holcomb announced NAMB's trustees will consider naming an interim president at its upcoming May 2 meeting as well as begin the search process for a new president.

In the meantime, Carlos Ferrer, NAMB's chief financial officer, who was named the previous week as the interim chief operating officer, would assume all executive leadership responsibilities, Holcomb said.

"Carlos is a man of great giftedness and integrity, and he will provide outstanding leadership during this time." Ferrer, a native of Cuba, joined the former Home Mission Board in 1992 as controller.

Reccord closed his remarks to the employees affirming his own confidence in the SBC's domestic mission board.

"Southern Baptists everywhere can be proud of their North American Mission Board's effectiveness and efficiencies. They can be proud of their missionaries," Reccord said. "They can give with confidence that tremendous financial efficiencies have been achieved as a result of the denomination's restructuring and a conscientious staff's diligent efforts."

WWW.BPNEWS.NET
Copyright (c) 2001 - 2006 Southern Baptist Convention, Baptist Press
From Baptist Press website, FAQ: Can I reprint BP stories?
Churches and individuals are permitted to use Baptist Press copy, unaltered, with attribution made to Baptist Press.

Appendix 3   Christian Index Article: "North American Missions: Hanging in the Balance"

North America: Hanging in the balance

An Analysis

By Joe Westbury, Managing Editor, with additional reporting by J. Gerald Harris, Editor
Published: February 16, 2006

Expectations were high in 1997 when the North American Mission Board was forged out of three previous Southern Baptist entities during the ambitious Covenant for a New Century restructuring. Increased operational efficiencies from the merger into NAMB were projected to allow Southern Baptists to be more effective than ever in impacting the United States and Canada with the Gospel.

But nine years into the venture, Georgia Baptist pastors are wondering if those expectations have been met. More importantly, new initiatives in evangelism and church planting have failed to produce the anticipated results – and the denomination's total of funded career missionaries has declined by 10 percent.

While NAMB admittedly has a full plate with its program assignments, it stands unique among Southern Baptist agencies because of three responsibilities – it is the only agency charged with developing and implementing a national strategy for evangelism and church planting, and is solely responsible for the care and nurture of the North American missionary force.

NAMB stands at a critical milestone as it enters its 10th year this summer. Onlookers at the state and national level will be looking closely to see if the agency can reverse the course in those three critical areas of effectiveness.

A letter to our readers

As Georgia Baptists we are fortunate to have one of Southern Baptists' premier agencies located in our state.

The Christian Index has always been a strong supporter of the North American Mission Board and we are proud to have it as a partner in our joint calling to win our state and North America to Christ. This special report, written at the request of many pastors over a several month period, seeks to address some concerns of how the agency is working to reach the lost for Christ.

We want to affirm our commitment to NAMB and especially to our missionaries. We encourage all Georgia Baptists to sacrificially give to this year's Annie Armstrong Easter Offering so NAMB can be more effective than ever in taking the Gospel to a hurting world.

J. Gerald Harris
Editor

NAMB's report card is not all gloom and doom. For example, there are bright spots and phenomenal gains in World Changers involvement, chaplaincy enlistment, and disaster relief participation – which is coordinated by NAMB but staffed by state convention volunteers. But other areas are a mixed bag. Missions education continues to take it on the chin and FamilyNet struggles to be less of a cash drain.

But it's those three key areas of evangelism, church planting and missionary recruitment that define the agency in the eyes of most Southern Baptists.

"What Now?" ... and "Who Cares?"

Last year was to be the year of jubilation in Southern Baptist life as the denomination celebrated the historic starting of 2,500 congregations and the baptism of a record 1 million new believers.

Instead it was glossed over as a year of no particular importance in denominational milestones. Church starts came in at 1,636 and baptisms will most likely hover around 390,000.

But that's not the way it was meant to be.

In January 2003 NAMB announced the launch of the most extensive evangelistic campaign in SBC history. It was billed as the denomination's response to the widespread soul searching which the nation was experiencing following the terrorist attacks of 9/11.

The "What Now?" campaign, tailored for both America and Canada, was built on a three-year strategy for personal revival and national spiritual awakening. The outreach would culminate with the largest national media campaign in Southern Baptist history – a million dollar extravaganza of television, radio, periodicals, and Internet advertising designed to get the attention of millions who do not attend church or are not immediately receptive to the Gospel.

Tens of thousands of dollars were spent on the publication of leadership materials by NAMB as well as state conventions who were gearing up to prepare their laity for the campaign. In Georgia, statewide meetings called Wave Revivals were organized in expectation of tying into the national media blitz that would undergird the efforts of the local church.

But the campaign failed to coalesce and – halfway into the effort – funding was pulled. The only problem was that this important decision was not uniformly communicated to state conventions. And some state papers, like the *Index*, continued to publicize the national campaign for nearly a year after its demise.

It was a good idea with a poor execution, observers say.

The biggest holdover from the campaign – the million baptisms – was resurrected last summer when SBC President Bobby Welch, who sensed a lack of emphasis on evangelism, launched his "'Everyone Can' Kingdom Challenge." Without his emphasis on a million baptisms, Southern Baptists would currently have no national evangelistic stack pole.

But in the summer of 2005 – during the same SBC annual meeting when Welch was launching his million baptism theme – NAMB launched a new, improved evangelism initiative. Titled "Who Cares?" – and sometimes referred to as "See Who Cares" – the campaign was launched with the usual normal fanfare.

NAMB President Bob Reccord announced the new media campaign would be launched "this fall" with a variety of television commercials dealing with life issues. But as of next week – eight months to the day when it was announced on June 21 – there is still no sign of a campaign. No billboards. No newspaper ads. No radio or television spots.

Chuck Allen, NAMB chief operating officer, told the Index the rollout had been delayed due to the Gulf Coast hurricanes, overloading NAMB staff with other responsibilities. But the campaign was not being produced by NAMB staff, having been outsourced to InovaOne, a new vendor.

That arrangement would not have affected NAMB's personnel who were responding to disaster relief. In reality the new start-up company, which was already producing NAMB's video coverage of disaster relief response, did not have adequate staff to operate on both fronts. Something had to give, and it was the evangelism launch, according to Allen's explanation.

Some observers say Southern Baptists lost a golden opportunity to capitalize on the disasters by not holding to the original launch date. They say the agency had a captive audience ready to hear the message – evacuees scattered throughout several states, traumatized and asking hard questions of God. Add to those numbers the millions who watched the televised accounts around North America and there was a harvest for the taking.

No other denomination was poised to make such an evangelistic impact. But the moment was lost.

One of Allen's explanations for the agency pulling the "What Now?" campaign – the proliferation of SBC themes in the denominational martketplace such as Act 1:8 and Empowering Kingdom Growth – is a little weak because those themes remain in abundance. With the launch of the new campaign, Southern Baptists will simply replace "What Now?" with "Who Cares?" in the crowded marketplace of themes.

What year is it – 2000 or 2006?

Though NAMB's latest evangelistic endeavor is still waiting in the wings, it has had a Web presence for several months. Its Web site may be open for business but it's clearly not ready for prime time.

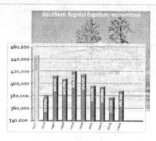

Chart about "Southern Baptist baptism momentum" and related information: http://www.christianindex.org/2016.article

When someone surfs the Net and visits the site at www.seewhocares.com they view the material and then are prompted to call a toll free number [1 (888) 537-8720] for spiritual assistance. But the recorded voice says "Thank you for calling the Jesus 2000 phone line ..."

That was the counseling phone number used by the Celebrate Jesus 2000 evangelism emphasis at the turn of the millennium – and predated the ill-fated "What Now?" campaign by five years. That error – simply failing to update a voice message five years after it expired – flies in the face of NAMB's newly stated desire to be "world class" in all that it does. That new concept of being "world class" is one of the driving reasons for outsourcing work to InovaOne and other vendors, but it's been an elusive concept to define.

The agency's role as a catalyst for revival

The lack of a consistent evangelism strategy for the SBC has not helped to bolster the denomination's shrinking baptism levels. Admittedly, North Americans live in an increasingly hostile environment toward spiritual matters and national revival will require divine intervention. But denominations see themselves as a catalyst in the process and are the primary champions for casting the vision for an ongoing emphasis on personal and corporate evangelism.

In July 2004, Reccord told participants at NAMB's Summer State Leadership Conference in Orlando that "in the next 12-18 months the United States no longer will claim a majority of Americans who identify with the Protestant faith."

If his timeline is correct, we just passed that threshold. The need for a coordinated national evangelism strategy has never been greater.

A self-funded missionary force

How many North American missionaries are currently on the field? It depends on how you count them. NAMB, through Baptist Press and other outlets, regularly states that more than 5,300 North American missionaries are funded through the Annie Armstrong Easter Offering (AAEO). But a closer look shows NAMB is throwing some apples in with the oranges, placing them in a blender, and still calling the mixture orange juice.

According to information supplied by NAMB based on the most recent headcount as of Dec. 31, there are 5,364 North American missionaries. However, only 2,942 are funded by the AAEO. The remaining 2,422 – or 45 percent – are self-funded volunteers serving through the Mission Service Corps. See chart on page 13.

While volunteers are a vital part of the missionary force they do not receive housing, salary, benefits, or any other financial support from Annie. They raise all of their salary by being bivocational or by soliciting friends and family – a throwback to the missionary society approach before the days of the Cooperative Program.

Chart: "Are Southern Baptists moving toward a self-funded missionary force?" and related information: http://www.christianindex.org/2018.article

When they were founded in 1977, MSC workers were categorized as volunteers, which separated them from their funded brethren. To avoid any confusion the Home Mission Board included them in the total count but kept the volunteer designation. Volunteers had to serve a minimum of two years before they were listed in the missionary personnel count.

NAMB, on the other hand, removed the volunteer status, lowered the service requirement to only four months and commissioned them as full-blooded missionaries – which blurred the line of who's who in the headcount. And therein lies the rub.

NAMB's missionary headcount has been growing because of those who come into and out of the force as volunteers. As far as being included in the headcount goes, a retired couple who drives around the American West to encourage missionaries is on the same footing as a seminary trained couple who have been serving 10 years.

And, while they do receive some training from NAMB, it does not come from AAEO gifts.

A further look at the figures reveals a disturbing trend: Under NAMB's administration, the funded career missionary headcount has actually declined by 329 between NAMB's first year and Dec. 31, 2005 – a full 10 percent – while the MSC volunteers have jumped by 827, or 34 percent.

To put it in layman's terms, nearly half of today's North American missionary force is funded by individuals in churches (friends and family) who may or may not be redirecting missions dollars from Annie to support those who are more eloquent speakers when they come asking for dollars. MSC [volunteers] cannot directly solicit funds from churches but they can accept funds if they are offered.

That was the common approach Southern Baptists used for decades and why the Cooperative Program was founded – churches pooling their dollars to fund an army of missionaries. But the old adage that Southern Baptist missionaries are more effective because they don't have to return home to raise their support is no longer absolute truth. At least, not as long as Mission Service Corps are included in their ranks.

The International Mission Board, on the other hand, does not include any volunteers in its headcount. While it is far more expensive to place international missionaries on the field, the IMB has still been able to outstrip NAMB in the number of funded missionaries.

Comparing the same time frame – from 1997 when NAMB was founded until December 2005, NAMB's headcount of funded missionaries actually dropped 329 or 10 percent, as previously stated. But the IMB's headcount jumped 917 to 5,165, according to Scott Holste, IMB associate vice president for research and strategic services.

International missionaries have always been the perceived favorites of the Southern Baptist missionary efforts, perhaps due to the lure of the foreign and the remote. But while the IMB has received substantially more funds due to higher overseas operating costs and currency fluctuations, it still has similar expenses as NAMB such as escalating medical costs and retirement benefits which constantly erode those funds. Yet, they are still able to grow their missionary ranks through priority funding.

Reaching a Bold Mission Thrust Goal – with gratitude to MSC

In a January 21, 2000, Baptist Press story, NAMB stated that it had reached the Bold Mission Thrust goal of 5,000 missionaries, right on schedule. But that total reflected the established practice of including MSC, which gave Southern Baptists a false sense of accomplishment.

Bill Graham, then-manager of NAMB's missionary personnel unit, attributed much of the increase "to more dollars made available for missionary support because of efficiencies gained from the restructuring of the SBC in 1997.

"The intent of that restructuring has been to put money forward in the field, and I think we are seeing the results of that action. And the commitment that the agency is making is showing up in the numbers," he said.

But that momentum in funding career missionaries seems to have been short-lived.

James DotsonBP

NAMB pressed a fire truck into service to promote its campus Elevate leadership conferences. It lost $600,000 in its first year and never broke even, though it was expected to be a significant source of revenue.

Increased efficiency

Two years later at the June 2002 meeting of the Southern Baptist Convention, NAMB President Bob Reccord gave a progress report on the first five years of the agency's existence. The committee leading the SBC restructure anticipated $34 million in savings during those early years.

"I'm here to tell you we didn't make it – we surpassed it" by $6 million, "redirecting to front-line ministries a total of $40,387,000," he said.

The redirected funds, he said, made possible Strategic Focus Cities church planting and evangelism efforts ($14.1 million), the Nehemiah Project ($7.3 million) training and mentoring program for church planters and other ministries. But the efficiencies attributed by Bill Graham that were directed to missionary support in those early years has not carried over to future years.

And while NAMB has lower overhead, it has also been able to draw down the cash reserves it received from the former Home Mission Board at its founding. In 1997 NAMB began with a $55 million cash cushion for emergency operating costs. The balance, according to the 2004 SBC annual, is $23 million – a decrease of $32 million in 7 years.

Belt tightening ... and belt loosening

NAMB has apparently swung between periods of erratic belt tightening and loosening. For example, in August 2003 it announced it was trimming its 2004 budget by 6 percent, eliminating 31 positions and reducing program support due to a softening economy.

But the following year, when staff were being asked to do more with less, NAMB launched the first of five college leadership conferences called Elevate.

NAMB confirmed to the *Index* that the 2004 conferences lost more than $600,000. But rather than canceling the two conferences scheduled for 2005 it held the course, losing so much on the first conference that it cancelled the second just weeks before it was ready to begin. A fifth conference in the series, set for next month in Atlanta, has already been cancelled.

Another expenditure was the creation of a high-tech walk-through exhibit called the Vision Center, which was constructed in NAMB's lobby. Modeled after a similar interactive information center at Focus on the Family, the three-dimensional, interactive experience of sight, sound, and touch using ultra-realistic professionally-designed sets was built, sources say, at a cost of $1 million.

The exhibit was debuted during the 1999 SBC meeting in Atlanta and was the crown jewel in NAMB's early years. But the repeat crowds failed to materialize and the center was shut down four years later.

Church planting numbers slow to grow

A look at church planting numbers shows a similar period of less than stellar growth for NAMB, given the efficiencies that were expected. As recent as the Feb. 8 meeting of NAMB's board of trustees Reccord reiterated that comparable overhead between it and the three agencies it replaced had dropped from 25 percent in 1996 to less than 12 percent today.

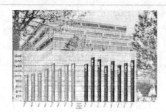

Chart about "Southern Baptist church plants" and related information: http://www.christianindex.org/2017.article

SBC church planting increased slowly yet consistently for the eight years prior to NAMB's launch. Under NAMB, congregational starts have been on a roller coaster ride. It's most recent year shows an increase of 132 church plants from the Home Mission Board's final year of 1996. See chart on page 12.

The most significant increase was for the years of 1999 and 2000 following Reccord's announcement of providing an additional $2 million for church planting and evangelism. When those one-time funds were put on the field, results were almost immediate – church plants jumped 258 to a record 1,747 in the first year and baptisms jumped 12,078.

But when the funds were depleted, the momentum ceased and growth came to a standstill.

Like evangelism, church planting is an increasingly difficult assignment in a post-modern world and the work is not to be taken lightly. Strong churches make a strong society, but Baptists remain weak in showing sustained growth.

InovaOne

In early 2003 NAMB brought in Steve Sanford, said to be a personal friend of Reccord from their days in Virginia, to conduct an audit of NAMB's media strategy. The repercussions from that audit continue to reverberate throughout the agency to this day.

Sanford presented the audit to Reccord in the Fall of 2003. When the dust had settled, 40 positions were eliminated and 31 employees were terminated before the Thanksgiving and Christmas holiday season. And, by coincidence or not, much of the work was handed off to InovaOne – a perceived conflict of interest for a consultant to directly benefit from an audit he conducted.

While InovaOne's own case study details the 2003 timeline of the study, a check with Georgia Secretary of State Cathy Cox's Web site shows the company was not registered in the state until the following year – on Dec. 1, 2004. In fact, Sanford registered three other business entities on the same day: InovaOne Aviation, InovaOne Enterprises, and InovaOne Strategies.

While Chuck Allen defends InovaOne (www.inovaone.com) as simply a transition company helping NAMB outsource the workload, employees feel their jobs are slowly going to a secular company that was created to take away their ministries. That corporate mindset, they say, has permeated NAMB's culture since it was founded. NAMB has maintained that it is not a church but a business, and will operate as a business.

The final sentence in the InovaOne case study of the audit, which was downloaded from its Web site, paints a dim future for NAMB staff: "It (NAMB) is now well-positioned to operate with a substantially reduced head count and more cost-effective communication systems."

The bulk of the fall terminations removed many long-term employees from NAMB's ranks, some with more than 25 years experience with former agencies such at the Home Mission Board and Brotherhood Commission. Gone were the editors/writers, graphic designers, and video production team.

NAMB's newest evangelism initiative, called "Who Cares?," will be nearly a year behind schedule when it launches this summer.

If InovaOne is just one of many vendors NAMB is using, the agency has certainly developed a strong affinity for its products. Reccord endorses the company – a secular for-profit entity – as an equal partner in its "Who Cares?" evangelistic campaign (www.seewhocares.org/) and Reccord, NAMB Chief Counsel Randy Singer, and Mike Carlisle, vice president of strategic communications, have offered similar endorsements at the InovaOne home page. But NAMB has not been as generous – or at least not as public – with praise for the printers who produce their magazines or airlines with whom they partner through negotiated group fares.

Shifting jobs to InovaOne

Throughout 2005 InovaOne began taking on more of NAMB's workload and was given the contract to produce the "Who Cares?" evangelism strategy and the new 316 Network – both of which Reccord unveiled in June at the SBC annual meeting.

And in December InovaOne produced NAMB's first video Christmas greeting from Bob and Cheryl Reccord, which is still available for viewing at: www.inovamedia.com/president_christmas_card/video.nocss.html?tr=y&auid=1277734.

But NAMB is a little inconsistent in its explanation of the outsourcing, at least as it relates to its video production. In an interview with the *Index*, Allen said it was becoming too expensive for NAMB to stay current with ever-changing video production technology. But during the interview he admitted that NAMB was updating its basement production studio to expand onsite recording – without a staff to run the equipment. Observers say it would seem inconsistent to use mission dollars to update a studio if NAMB was wanting to get out of the video production business.

InovaOne, who has already been working in the studio, is the obvious frontline candidate to provide the manpower. And the longer NAMB waits to dispose of the equipment, the less valuable it becomes – another inconsistency in its business plan.

Allen also said there was a strong possibility that NAMB would someday sell off all of the production equipment to an outside vendor and close the studio completely. But on Feb. 9 he affirmed that all of the equipment purchased with Cooperative Program dollars belongs to NAMB and none has been sold.

But if the equipment belongs to NAMB and is just used by InovaOne – and other outside vendors – employees are confused about why the area has become restricted while InovaOne employees roam freely. Locks have been changed and NAMB employees no longer have unlimited access to the area.

If NAMB believes secular outside vendors such as InovaOne can do a better job of communicating its message to churches than Southern Baptist employees on staff, InovaOne's case study should raise a red flag. Its first paragraph identifies NAMB's audience as *"43,000 churches, 1,200 local organizations, 42 state conventions, and tens of thousands of missionaries throughout the United States and Canada."*

The "1,200 local organizations" should be more correctly identified as Baptist associations – and the missionary count is "tens of thousands" more than the 5,364 currently employed. It appears that InovaOne has a problem defining NAMB's identity in its own audit report.

Promise Keepers

A primary focus of NAMB has been "partnerships" with like-minded evangelical groups. NAMB has branched out of the Southern Baptist fold to embrace ministry options with groups such as Focus on the Family, Campus Crusade, and others with proven benefits.

But it has sometimes been difficult to determine when its president has been speaking for NAMB or for his own personal ministry, Total Life Impact. The ministry, which lists Reccord and wife Cheryl as motivational speakers, sells a variety of their books and $49 custom-made plaques for children's rooms.

Allen defends Reccord's speaking engagements – especially one at Focus on the Family where the couple's appearance was reported by a Baptist Press story. Allen maintains that Reccord keeps a clear separation between what is a NAMB-related speaking engagement and what is his personal ministry. But if the couple were speaking as private individuals, it would not be necessary for Baptist Press to run a story on their appearance.

Reccord's speaking engagements have been prolific but they may not have all been to promote North American missions. For example, he has spoken on the Focus on the Family national radio program, was featured at Promise

Keepers, has been a guest on *The 700 Club* and granted interviews to publications such as *Today's Pentecostal Evangel*.

But on all of those – according to their Web sites – he has spoken on general topics such as how to raise your children and safeguard your marriage against infidelity. Topics well and good, as affirmed in NAMB's staff policy manual, but not necessarily in keeping with the agency's primary objectives.

According to the policy manual in relation to when honoraria can be accepted, "... *messages on marriage, general leadership issues, ethics, sexual purity, etc. may be good topics but are not considered a reflection of NAMB's six MMOs* (Major Missions Objectives)."

The conflict, for many, comes when Reccord speaks on those topics and promotes his own books and the ministry's Web site at www.totallifeimpact.com. If he is introduced as president of NAMB it would be expected that he would be an advocate for the mission agency's family evangelism unit. But such is not always the case.

So, when is Reccord speaking on behalf of NAMB and when is he speaking on behalf of his and his wife's ministry? That's difficult to determine.

Some observers question the wisdom of such a move, even if Total Life Impact lists his wife as president rather than himself. The ministry, they say, is in conflict with NAMB's family evangelism unit and undermines that unit's effectiveness. They maintain that Delta Air Lines would not allow CEO Jerry Grinstein to set up a personal charter jet service that would compete with the airline's day-to-day operations, so why should NAMB allow any employee to launch a business that competes with the agency's objectives?

The waters will become even muddier this summer as Reccord speaks at all 19 Promise Keepers rallies nationwide. He has already told staff that he has reworked his schedule to accommodate the request and may be unavailable for any additional NAMB speaking engagements for that time frame – nearly half of the year's Friday evenings.

While NAMB board members have not questioned the move, it may not be the gold mine for Southern Baptists that Reccord alleges it will be. Justifying the engagement at NAMB's board meeting on Feb. 8 he told trustees that 56 percent of Promise Keepers attendees have a Southern Baptist affiliation – implying that the men are just the market to hear his message and be ushered into an on mission lifestyle.

But when contacted by the *Index*, Steve Chavis, communications director for Promise Keepers, painted a slightly different picture.

"We don't actually break the denominations down by individual groups," he said. "But our research shows that 25 percent of our attendees claim some kind of Baptist affiliation. That includes all groups across the Baptist spectrum – Southern, American, National, whatever."

NAMB's staffing levels have gone through waves of restructuring and downsizing. The Dec. 2, 2005 telephone list shows the fall vacancies versus levels two years ago.

Chavis then added that the next largest category chosen by participants is "non-denomination" with a 24 percent affiliation.

Based on those figures, instead of speaking to a group that is 56 percent Southern Baptist, Reccord will actually be speaking to a group of whom at least 75% are *not* Southern Baptist.

Looking to the future

What does the future hold for NAMB and the Southern Baptist Convention? Allen does not believe there will be any more terminations for 2006 on the scale of past years. He states the headcount will remain where it is without substantial reduction in the workforce. And, he adds, he does not believe many employees are actually fearful for their jobs – regardless of the InovaOne audit report on the need for outsourcing.

NAMB remains the primary agency to lead the denomination forward in implementing a national strategy in evangelism and church planting. And while the missionary force continues to grow through volunteer labor – the future of its funded career force may continue to slide without increased giving to the Annie Armstrong Easter Offering.

But the long-term implications are even more critical to the future of the International Mission Board. If church planting and evangelism continue their slide there will be fewer congregations being birthed that support the Cooperative Program and related offerings. And with a slide in offerings, international missions may find itself on the ropes. The bottom line is that if we lose the homeland, we lose the world.

Appendix 4 Letter Affirming Bob Reccord, signed by 41 SBC Leaders

Reccord supporters release statement about NAMB work and leader's integrity

Statement of Support

In recent days, the leadership, character and integrity of our friend, Dr. Bob Reccord, has been the subject of controversy. The purpose of this letter is to express our support for Bob as a godly man of uncompromising integrity.

We love Bob as a friend, have had a chance to ask him questions about the events reported in the media, and have heard him share his heart. He has acted with integrity and character throughout his nine year tenure as NAMB's President and never more so than in these last tumultuous weeks. Where he has made misjudgments, he has freely acknowledged them and assumed responsibility. But these are mistakes of the head, not the heart – the kinds of misjudgments that innovative leaders make in an effort to accomplish things that have never been done before.

They by no means negate Bob's demonstrated commitment to lead with integrity nor the accomplishments we've seen under his leadership at NAMB.

Bob's visionary leadership, both as chairman of the task force that led the implementation of the restructuring of the Southern Baptist Convention and as President of NAMB, has re-energized many and resulted in significant new initiatives that will have a permanent impact on the face of North American missions.

He led Southern Baptists into an unprecedented focus on reaching our large metropolitan areas, resulting in more than 320 healthy new church starts in strategic cities alone.

His vision launched the Nehemiah church planting partnership with each of our SBC seminaries, training hundreds of new church planters to reach the most desperate areas of our continent.

He provided the impetus for growing the World Changers program – high school students rehabilitating inner city homes – from a total of 9,000 students before NAMB was formed to nearly 25,000 students now.

He led the charge in overseeing unprecedented disaster relief efforts by Southern Baptists, who brought hope and help to New York residents after 9/11 and were widely recognized as one of the few bright spots in the aftermath of Hurricanes Katrina, Rita and Wilma.

And, through increased efficiencies at NAMB, he saw to it that millions of additional dollars went into the mission field through state cooperative budgets and new initiatives than would have been available if the restructuring had not occurred.

In addition to these tangible results, we affirm those intangible characteristics we see in Bob that are harder to measure – a tireless work ethic, the courage to try innovative new approaches (such as a conference to reach young professionals), doctrinal integrity and a passion to reach North America. We also affirm his spiritual walk and his ability to communicate the good news in ways relevant to those outside Southern Baptist circles. And we see these same characteristics of godliness and integrity displayed in the life of his wife Cheryl and in her conduct through these circumstances.

Despite our belief in Bob's leadership, we recognize that the President and the Board of Trustees of any organization must be of like mind both philosophically and methodologically. Sometimes honest differences of opinion about leadership style or strategy dictate the need for change. We also recognize that the need to stand firm on convictions is not necessarily the same as the desire to stand firm for the sake of a position.

We therefore respect and affirm Bob's decision to step down as President of NAMB for the sake of the Agency and its more than 5,000 missionaries. In fact, this action heightens our respect for his character and demonstrates his willingness to do what is best for the Kingdom even if it results in personal sacrifice.

We believe these circumstances have been used by God to forge Bob for even greater ministry in the days ahead. We pledge our support to help make that happen. And we remain proud to call him a friend and the founding President of the North American Mission Board.

Sincerely,

Mark Brister, President, Oklahoma Baptist University, Shawnee, Okla.

Michael Catt, Senior Pastor, Sherwood Baptist Church, Albany, Ga.

David Clippard, Executive Director, Missouri Baptist Convention

Brent Crowe, national student conference speaker

Steve Davis, Executive Director, State Convention of Baptists in Indiana

Michael Dean, Senior Pastor, Travis Avenue Baptist Church, Ft. Worth, Tx.

Ronnie Floyd, Senior Pastor, First Baptist Church, Springdale, Ark.

Danny Forshee, seminary professor and conference speaker, Ft. Worth, Tx.

Rob Futral, Senior Pastor, Broadmoor Baptist Church, Madison, Miss.

Tim Groshans, Student Leadership University, Orlando, Fla.

Jack Graham, Senior Pastor, Prestonwood Baptist Church, Dallas, Tx and former President of SBC

Michael Hamlet, Senior Pastor, First Baptist Church, North Spartanburg, S. C.

Dean Haun, Senior Pastor, First Baptist Church, Jonesboro, Ga.

Jim Henry, former Senior Pastor, First Baptist Church, Orlando, Fla. and former President of SBC

Johnny Hunt, Senior Pastor, First Baptist Church, Woodstock, Ga.

Anthony Jordan, Executive Director, Oklahoma Baptist Convention

Tony Lambert, Senior Pastor, Crossgates Baptist Church, Brandon, Miss.

Michel Lewis, Senior Pastor, Great Hills Baptist Church, Austin, Tx.

David McKinnley, Sr. Assoc.Pastor, Prestonwood Baptist Church, Dallas, Tx.

James Merritt, Senior Pastor, CrossPoint Community Church, and former President of SBC

Hollie Miller, Senior Pastor, Sevier Heights Baptist Church, Knoxville, Tenn.

Kendall Moore, Attorney and trustee for Family Net TV

Forest Pollock, Senior Pastor, Bell Shoals Baptist Church, Brandon, Fla.

Richard Powell, Senior Pastor, McGregor Baptist Church, Ft. Myers, Fla.

Ike Reighard, Chief People Officer, HomeBanc Corp,, Atlanta, Ga.

Russell Shinpock, Senior Pastor, First Baptist Church, Snellville, Ga.

Jay Strack, Pres./CEO Student Leadership University, Orlando, Fla.

Jerry Sutton, Senior Pastor, Two Rivers Baptist Church, Nashville, Tenn.

Claude Thomas, Equip Ministries, Atlanta, Ga.

Eric Thomas, Senior Pastor, First Baptist Church, Norfolk, Va.

Keith Thomas, Senior Pastor, Cottage Hill Baptist Church, Mobile, Ala.

Ted Traylor, Senior Pastor, Olive Baptist Church, Pensacola, Fla.

David Uth, Senior Pastor,First Baptist Church, Orlando, Florida

Jerry Vines, Former Senior Pastor, First Baptist Church, Jacksonville, Fla. and former President of the SBC

Ken Whitten, Senior Pastor, Idlewild Baptist Church, Tampa, Fla.

Hayes Wicker, Senior Pastor, First Baptist Church, Naples, Fla.

Don Wilton, Senior Pastor, First Baptist Church, Spartanburg, S. C.

Larry Wynn, Senior Pastor, Senior Pastor, Hebron Baptist Church, Dacula, Ga.

Danny Wood, Senior Pastor, Shades Mountain Baptist Church, Birmingham, Ala.

Bryant Wright, Senior Pastor, Johnson Ferry Baptist Church, Marietta, Ga., and current President, SBC Pastors' Conference

H. Edwin Young, Senior Pastor, Second Baptist Church, Houston, Tx and former President of the SBC

Posted on several websites and reported by *Baptist Press News*, www.bpnews.net, April 24 2006.

Appendix 5 Waiver NAMB Staff Were Required to Sign When They Left

RELEASE AND WAIVER AGREEMENT

In consideration of the enhanced separation benefits that The North American Mission Board of the Southern Baptist Convention, Inc. (hereinafter collectively "NAMB") offered to me in writing and in further consideration of the sum of ten ($10.00) dollars and other good and valuable consideration, the receipt and sufficiency of which are hereby acknowledged, I hereby release and discharge NAMB, and any corporate entity into which NAMB may be merged or consolidated, its officers, agents, directors and employees, from any and all claims, losses or expenses I may have had, or may later claim to have had, against them for personal injuries, backpay, losses, or damages to me or my property, or any other losses or expenses of any kind resulting from anything which has occurred up until the present time, including, but not limited to, claims arising out of my employment, or the termination of my employment with NAMB. I understand that by signing this Agreement and accepting the enhanced separation benefits package, I am waiving any rights to pursue any individual claim against NAMB, and any corporate entity into which NAMB may be merged or consolidated, its directors, officers, agents or employees, in any state or federal court or before any state or federal agency, including for examples, the Equal Employment Opportunity Commission of the Department of Labor, for backpay, severance pay, liquidated damages, losses or other damages to me or my property resulting from any claimed violation of state or federal law: including, for example, claims arising out of Title VII of the Civil Rights Act of 1964, (prohibiting discrimination on the basis of sex, national origin, color, race or religion); claims arising under the Age Discrimination in Employment Act of 1967 (prohibiting discrimination on account of age); claims arising out of the American with Disabilities Act, (prohibiting discrimination on the basis of disabilities); claims arising under the Family and

Medical Leave Act; or any other federal or state law pertaining to employment or employee benefits.

I covenant and agree that all monies received under this Agreement will become immediately due and payable to NAMB if I should ever disavow this Agreement, breach any term of this Agreement, or if the Agreement is found to be unenforceable.

I further agree to maintain the confidentiality of this Agreement and its terms, including but not limited to the consideration provided for, and to make no statement or to take any action which would result in any publicity or disclosure concerning this Agreement. Additionally, I agree to keep confidential all aspects of my employment relationship with NAMB, except for disclosures compelled by legal process and agree not to divulge or use any confidential information obtained in the course of my employment with NAMB to the detriment of NAMB. I further agree to make no public or private statements or disclosures concerning my employment or treatment by NAMB or any of its officers, directors, or employees, and not to portray them in a negative or poor light to anyone. NAMB and I shall have the right to disseminate information concerning the Agreement in order for NAMB to implement its provisions and for me to manage my normal business affairs. Failure to comply with any provisions of this Agreement shall constitute a material breach of this Agreement.

Appendix 6 Steve Stanford's Web Response to Index Article

InovaOne Response to Christian Index article 'North America: Hanging in the Balance'

Under normal circumstances InovaOne and founder Steve Sanford would not acknowledge mud-slinging from tabloid journalism, but due to the malicious nature of the article, the blatant misrepresentations and inaccuracies contained therein, and the fact that the attacks are from Christian press, the following response is offered.

InovaOne Studios is outraged and disappointed that the (Georgia) Christian Index would resort to what amounts to nothing more than tabloid journalism by (a) running a negative attack against the North American Mission Board, SBC (NAMB) using InovaOne in a fabricated and inaccurate smoking gun portrayal against NAMB; (b) using its portrayal of InovaOne as the means to attack the personal credibility of Dr. Robert Reccord, President of the North American Mission Board, SBC; (c) defaming the character of Steve Sanford using un-cited, anonymous and fabricated sources to support inaccuracies and unsubstantiated innuendo; (d) refusing to provide any notification or opportunity for InovaOne or Sanford to be interviewed or respond to the baseless accusations; and (e) seeking to destroy the integrity and mission of a company that has a Christian management team by using the term 'Secular,' as if to suggest that any for-profit company is somehow un-Christian.

To label this article as an "analysis" is nothing more than a smokescreen to cover sub-standard and shoddy journalistic practices and reporting that appears to be motivated by some personal agenda of the writer to destroy the incredible work that NAMB has done and continues to do. The real investigation here should be into the writer's motives and the anonymous sources who cowardly hide their identities while issuing defamatory and untruthful statements.

If Christian journalism is expected to be held to a higher standard than traditional mainstream 'secular media,' the

Christian Index has tarnished the ethical and moral image of the industry by publishing an article filled with such bias, fallacy and innuendo. Sanford notes that "I have had numerous encounters with mainstream media in my career both positive and negative in tone, but I have never seen any writer in the media be this unprofessional and lacking of journalistic skill and ethical standards." It is the hope of InovaOne that the Christian press at large will not continue to propagate this kind of shoddy journalism, but will instead seek the truth above a sensational story.

Appendix 7 Ardor Group Email

From: Tim Finley
Sent: Monday, September 13, 2004 12:56 PM
To: Allen, Chuck; Carlisle, Mike; Cogland, Mike; Harris, Richard; Yarbrough, John; Frost, Toby; Keesey, Doug; Lawson, Ron; Ebert, Mike; Reccord, Bob
Cc: 'mark arnold'; 'doug'
Subject: Ardor Group resignation letter

Monday September 13, 2004

TO:
North American Mission Board
Mike Carlisle
Chuck Allen
Mike Cogland
Richard Harris
John Yarbrough
Bob Reccord
Toby Frost
Doug Keesey
Ron Lawson and
Mike Ebert

FROM:
Ardor Group
Tim Finley
Mark Arnold
Doug Berg

Dear Brothers in Christ at North American Mission Board-

It is with great sadness that today the Ardor Group must write to inform you that we are respectfully withdrawing our creative estimate proposal and no longer desire to work on the "Now is the Time" media outreach project.

In April 2003 we initially came to Alpharetta to discuss your plans to execute a strategic outreach media campaign. At that first meeting, we were moved by your courage, vision and passion to launch out in new territory and to share the gospel through media not as you had done in the past but in a new fresh way. You told us of your plans to connect with non-believers outside the church with the gospel and you asked us to join you as partners in this effort.

17 months later, we believe this project no longer has any real vision or clarity. Ardor Group was hired because, as Dr. Reccord said in a future meeting with all of us attending, "Tim and Mark, we do not know how to talk to this culture outside the church, you do. Push us all the way to the cliff but not over. You do what you know how to do and let us handle the internal stuff with the churches at NAMB."

Sadly, we were never allowed to do what we are called to do and what we were originally hired to do. For 17 months we believe that we have been very, very patient through all the changes at NAMB. Changes in vision, mission, purpose and financial worries. Changes in leadership and constant management shuffling. We have waited and waited trying to keep our passion and enthusiasm hoping that it would all be worth it in the end. We believed strongly in our hearts that once all the shuffling and reorganization stopped and the right men were in the right positions, we would be able to produce television, radio, print, billboard, web sites and a giveaway booklet that would really bring lost and hurting men and women into the kingdom of God as we together communicated the gospel message in a fresh new wonderful way.

Now here we are in September 2004. The project is no longer, in our judgment, being led by any fresh breath of the Spirit of God. It is dull, stale and dead. Television commercials have been slashed from four to two. Billboards have been slashed. And the giveaway booklet is dead as well. All at the very last hour. And to top it all off you now want us to go back for a third time and redo our estimate and reduce the creative costs again for the remaining two television commercials.

We respectfully have had enough of all the changes. The last straw for us was when we heard the decision last week to go with a version of the "Power for Living" booklet as a giveaway item instead of producing a "Now is the Time" giveaway booklet specific to this media campaign. To now make that change as a giveaway item instead producing a focused follow-up giveaway specific to the campaign in our judgment just does not make any sense whatsoever. Sending a giveaway item to unchurched men and women that is not specific to how they were moved to respond in the first place will come across as bland and weird. It will not look cohesive to the entire campaign. And the effectiveness of the campaign will suffer greatly in purpose.

That NAMB decision "to just go with any old giveaway item to save costs" basically took all the wind out of our sails. It brought us back to square one and showed us that you are not really willing to take any risk at all and are not really committed to doing anything different. And thus, as we have said many times, if you are not going to do anything unique and relevant, you don't need us.

It seems that with every new month the scope of the project continued to decrease. At first it was an $11 million dollar media budget. Now it is around $360,000. With these limited resources, the media campaign will have little impact even if completed.

Mark Arnold, Doug Berg and I have been very impressed with the many wonderful things NAMB does to spread the gospel around the world. Although we wonder how much more could be done to further the gospel with NAMB's resources and talent if quick fearless decision making was at the core of your organizational leadership structure. If we might be so bold to suggest we see NAMB as an organizational nightmare as far as project decision making.

Again, we are saddened by our decision but we must move forward and work with other organizations that are spreading the gospel with a similar mindset and vision as ours. Our goal is to do that in a risky and cutting edge way that will cut through the secular clutter in the media. We have come to the conclusion that our goal is not shared by NAMB.

Even Paul and Peter did not see eye to eye for a time and had to travel their own separate ways to share the gospel the way they saw best. We just see things differently I guess and that is ok.

We wish you well.
God Bless You all,

Tim Finley
Mark Arnold
Doug Berg
ARDOR GROUP